D1708803

From the personal library collection of aviation history and memorabilia of Albert B. Eckerson Jr. (1918–1989).

Given by his son, Edwin T. Eckerson. 1992

Illustrated History of World War I in The Air

BOOKS WRITTEN OR EDITED BY STANLEY M. ULANOFF

Illustrated Guide to U. S. Missiles and Rockets
Fighter Pilot
MATS—The Story of the Military Air Transport Service
Bombs Away!
Military Miniature Handbook, with Wm. Imrie and Clyde Risley
The Unheard of American Ace, Capt. W. C. Lambert
Flying in Flanders, Lt. Willy Coppens
Illustrated History of World War I in the Air

AIR COMBAT CLASSICS

Winged Warfare, Lt. Col. William A. Bishop
Ace of Aces, Capt. René Fonck
Fighting Airman—The Way of the Eagle, Maj. Charles J. Biddle
Flying Fury, Maj. James T. B. McCudden
Wind in the Wires, Capt. Duncan Grinnell-Milne
The Red Baron, Capt. Manfred von Richthofen
Ace of the Iron Cross, Lt. Ernst Udet
Up and at 'Em, Lt. Col. Harold Hartney

Illustrated History of World War I in The Air

Stanley Ulanoff

Arco
New York

Published by ARCO PUBLISHING COMPANY, INC.
219 Park Avenue South, New York, N. Y. 10003

Library of Congress Number 69-100035

ISBN 0-668-01768-6

Printed in the United States of America

Foreword

VERY FEW photographs of aerial combat in World War I exist today, if they ever existed at all. There are a couple that are purported to be actual photos of a "dogfight," but their authenticity has been seriously questioned by a number of authorities. Needless to say, they are not color photographs, because the process had not yet been perfected at that time.

For the most part, however, the photos that do exist are static, generally depicting a plane and possibly the pilot, as in the classic photo of Eddie Rickenbacker next to his Spad, or a lineup of aircraft at an aerodrome. They did not have camera guns, and the cameras they did have were unable to capture action because there had not yet been produced lenses or shutters that were fast enough. Art, on the other hand, caught what the camera lens failed to get. The artist, who either witnessed the action himself or "used the eyes of the participant," put down on canvas all of the drama, color, and excitement of the event.

The art and photo coverage of the World War II was relatively total and complete, with the United States as well as foreign military services enlisting and commissioning into their ranks professional artists and photographers to depict all phases of the war in oil, watercolor, pen and ink, charcoal, photographs, and every other art medium. The work of a Farré, however, was certainly unique in World War I. At the time, there was little or no awareness on the part of the fighting powers, or perhaps no interest, to have that "war to end all wars" chronicled for posterity in an art form. So, with the exception of Farré's efforts—and those of some British artists, which fortunately were substantial—there are only a limited number of other fine examples of art work actually made during the conflict. These can be found at the *Musée de l'Air* in Paris, the Imperial War Museum in London, and other great national museums in Europe and the United States.

Illustrated History of World War I in the Air tells the story, through its illustrations, of the initial use of aircraft on a major scale in warfare. From time immemorial, battles were fought on the ground and on, or under, the sea. Infantrymen—foot soldiers—clashed in mortal combat. It didn't matter whether the weapon was a knife, a sword, a spear, a bow and arrow, or a rifle and bayonet. The mounted soldier then appeared on the scene as a more powerful war machine with greater mobility and range. At sea the oarsman gave way to sail, and the sail to steam. Later steam was replaced by the diesel engine, which also powered the submarine or U-boat. But an entirely new dimension was added when the fledgling "aeroplane," as it was then known, entered the lists.

The airplane of 1914 was a crude contraption, very little improved from that historic first Wright flyer of 1903. In fact, when war broke out the "aeroplane" was barely ten years old. At that time, the French as well as the British counted among their military aircraft the Blériot XI—the same model with which Louis Blériot, its builder, made the first historic crossing over the English Channel in 1909.

As the war progressed, the airplanes improved and so did the weapons they carried. By 1918, at the close of the war, scout or fighter planes were able to fly at 120 miles per hour. These "speed demons" included the French Spad XIII, the British Sopwith Camel and SE-5, and the German Fokker D VII.

During those four years of conflict many heroes flashed their deeds across the skies and over the Western Front. Some were great fighter aces like René Fonck, Billy Bishop, Jim McCudden, Manfred von Richthofen, and Eddie Rickenbacker. Others flew two-seater observation planes or bombers. Many were involved in colorful, dramatic "dog fights," or individual combat in the clouds.

This is the story of the first war in the air, a pictorial history of the air action in World War I, told through the various art media.

Acknowledgments

I WOULD like to acknowledge with gratitude Lt. Colonel Bob Webb and Mrs. Anna C. Urband of the Magazine Book Branch of the Office of the Assistant Secretary of Defense for Public Affairs who gave their wholehearted support to the writing of this book.

I am particularly grateful to Lt. Colonel John B. Devoe and William H. Winder of the Art and Museum Branch, Community Relations Division, Office of Information of the Secretary of the Air Force, for their splendid cooperation in giving permission for use of the Farré Collection and the six Clayton Knight paintings. I am also indebted to Lew Glaser and Howard E. Rieder of Revell, Inc. for their permission to use the splendid paintings of Jack Leynnwood and Brian Knight; to Abe Shikes and Dick Schwarzchild of Aurora Plastics Corp. for the use of their art; to L. S. Wetzel, Irving Lubow and Stan Harris of Renwal Products Inc. for allowing me to use the wonderful Gene Thomas and Mort Künstler paintings; to TRW Inc., M. A. Gentile, and Carol E. Kratovil for kindly giving permission to use some of Charles H. Hubbell's aviation art; to fellow "Cross & Cockade" member Joseph A. Phelan for the contribution of some of his fine work, and to Grosset & Dunlap for permission to reproduce this artwork; to Captain Eddie Rickenbacker for the use of the striking portrait of him by Howard Chandler Christy; to the RCAF for making available the portrait of Air Marshal Collishaw and Lt. Colonel Barker; to R. R. M. Ehrmann of Airfix Industries Ltd. for consenting to the reproduction of some of their fine illustrations; to my neighbor Cornell Jaray, publisher of Kennikat Press for the Vimnèra watercolors from *The Lafayette Flying Corps;* and to my good friend Clyde A. Risley of I/R Miniatures for the excellent pen-and-ink sketches he drew especially for this book.

With gratitude I acknowledge the assistance of my family, whose help was invaluable.

My appreciation also goes to Raoul Edward Holly, Keith Linde, and Alan Matcovsky for their help in typing the manuscript.

Contents

BOMBER AND RECONNAISSANCE AIRCRAFT

FLYING BOATS AND FLOATPLANES

BIOGRAPHICAL SKETCHES OF THE ARTISTS

Introduction

ARTILLERY SHELLS whistled over the lines of khaki clad men huddled in the muddy trenches below and continued on their way to crash with a resounding roar and an eruption of flame, earth, and rock among the soldiers in *feld grau* (field gray) in the woods beyond.

Battle-wise, the American troops, wearing flat steel helmets and with bayonets fixed, knew that the projectiles screaming overhead were friendly ones fired by their own artillery in support of the attack they were about to make on the Germans entrenched on the front.

Suddenly there was an ominous silence! The artillery fire had ceased. The shrill blast of a whistle rent the quiet, and the men in olive drab spewed forth from their muddy, rat-infested holes in the earth. "Over the top" they went. The Germans in their coal scuttle helmets were waiting for them in well-fortified positions in the woods. The staccato chatter of machine gun fire cut gaping holes in the lines of oncoming Allied troops, but on they came. Their numbers dwindled as comrades fell, but still they came forward, bayonets at the ready. The last few yards seemed an eternity but soon they were at the enemy positions. They jumped in, bayonets first—hand-to-hand—and the first line of trenches was theirs. In short order they took the next, and then the next line of trenches as the enemy fell back before the force of their ferocious onslaught.

And above the carnage of the battlefield, free as birds in the sky, wheeled the planes, their silver wings flashing gayly in the bright sun.

Fifty years have gone by since the close of the First World War.

Variously called "the war to end all wars" and "the war to save democracy," I have even heard it referred to as "the last of the fun wars" by a radio commentator. Whatever it was, World War I was far from "fun"—a great adventure, yes—but definitely not fun!

By no stretch of the imagination could anyone call amusing, living in mud and filth, in holes in the ground, for days on end, with the dead still lying where they fell, the stench of rot and putrification, rats, and the constantly gnawing body lice, called "cooties" by the men. And all of this notwithstanding, there was the ever-present threat of death. It was a risk to stick one's head over the parapet of the trench, not to mention the soldier's complete vulnerability, utterly exposed, in a frontal attack, or bayonet attack. Even in the relative safety of the trench protected from the direct fire of enemy rifles, pistols, and machine guns, he was the target of the indirect fire of mortars and artillery which had an arched trajectory and could drop a high explosive shell in on him. And, of course, there was the ever-present fear of poison gas. War, then, was the "Hell" that General Sherman described in the Civil War.

Ah, but this was the life of the infantryman—the "doughboy," the "poilu," and "Tommy Atkins."

It was true, there was another type of fighting man who lived in relatively clean quarters, slept in a bed, ate hot meals in a dining room, was able to keep himself and his clothes neat, away from the fire of the enemy. Moreover, this fellow soared above the clouds in the clean fresh air, free as a bird. This new breed of soldier was the flyer, the pilot, or military aviator. After he mastered the airplane, his war was in the air.

It was the mud that drove such men as Manfred *Frieherr* von Richthofen, better known as the "Red Baron," and Canadian ace Billy Bishop to seek transfers from the cavalry to their respective air services. Infantrymen like Americans Bill Thaw, Bert Hall, and Victor Chapman of the Foreign Legion quit the mud, filth, and the lice and rats of the trenches for the *Lafayette Escadrille* and the clean blue sky.

Although they sought respite from the mud and the dirt, they did not escape from death, for unfortunately death found them too, in the pure air above the white clouds. And death came in the same form that it did on the ground—a machine gun bullet that killed a pilot, or struck a vital part of the aircraft motor or controls and sent the plane crashing to the earth below. Allied fliers had the choice of riding their aircraft down to a crash or jumping to their deaths. (They were not equipped with parachutes as were the Germans toward the end of the war.) A more terrifying death for many World War I fliers was going down in flames! Regular machine-gun bullets or incendiary ones striking a plane's gas tank often ignited them, making a flaming pyre of the aircraft.

But this did not deter those intrepid fellows. They were a breed apart, true knights of the sky, whose steeds were frail aircraft of wood and canvas. Unlike their earthbound comrades below, theirs was a "clean" war and both sides lived by an unwritten chivalric code that rivaled that of King Arthur and his Knights of the Round Table. They formally challenged the adversary to individual combat above the clouds, saluted a gallant enemy, and dropped wreaths over the fallen foe's aerodrome.

Granted, there was an element of fun and certainly of adventure in flying, and even in facing the enemy in combat, chasing each other around the sky. But the fun ceased, at least for the chap on the receiving end, when the enemy had positioned himself, like glue, on his tail and proceeded to pour well-placed bursts of machine-gun fire into his aircraft. If he could not shake his adversary by skillful maneuvering, he ran a high risk of either spinning to earth out of control, crashing in flames, or of being killed outright by his enemy's machine gun.

As for the aircraft they flew, by today's standards they would be considered no more than frail box kites, which they closely resembled at the start of the war. This should not be regarded as strange, considering the fact that there was a span of little more than ten years from the invention of the airplane, in December 1903, to the outbreak of the Great War in August 1914. From that point on, however, one might say that the airplane really "took-off" and progressed rapidly in technological development.

Captain Duncan Grinnell-Milne, of the British Royal Flying Corps (RFC) and the Royal Air Force (RAF), described an episode in his book *Wind in the Wires* that resembled Rip Van Winkle's return from his long sleep. Grinnell-Milne had been captured by the Germans in December 1915 after a forced landing on the wrong side of the "lines." In May 1918 he had managed to return to England after escaping from the enemy. Before his capture, he had flown in such kitelike aircraft as the Caudron, and Maurice Farmans and had crash-landed in a slow lumbering B.E. 2C. The S.E.5's, Sopwith Camels, Spads and other relatively "high performance" aircraft were a revelation to him.

Major "Hap" Arnold, who was one day to command the greatest aggregate of air power in history, described the development cycle this way:

> One country would bring out a plane that could climb to a high altitude for fighting, only to see the plane of a hostile country far above it during a patrol. A designer in England would produce a plane having a speed of 115 miles an hour and believe that it was the fastest fighter on the battle front, only to hear that a German plane was much faster in a chase. Fighting in the air caused the production of very maneuverable, rapid-climbing, extra-strong planes. Bombing brought out large planes with a long radius of action, capable of carrying heavy loads. The types changed so fast that the best plane on the line one day might very well be called obsolete the next day. The resources of almost the entire world were engaged in producing the best possible aircraft, and the results achieved certainly justified the efforts expended.
>
> The increase in efficiency and the improvement in performance were obtained by taking advantage of all possible refinements in design and in securing better and more powerful engines. The airplanes at the end of the war by their performances dwarfed those produced before the war as a result of employing more efficient wing sections, a substantial reduction of head resistance, a decrease in the dead weight resulting from the use of stronger and lighter materials of construction, and as a result of having more reliable engines that weighed less per

> horsepower and using engines of much greater power.
>
> When a forced landing meant either the capture or death of the occupants of a plane, reliability was the principal qualification of an engine. Airplanes went out on missions and were continuously shot at by enemy planes and antiaircraft artillery. The strength of planes was increased to permit their having a good chance of returning safely even though some parts of the plane were destroyed. This necessitated an increase in the structural factor of safety. Bombers were sent on missions many hundred miles away from their bases, requiring very large fuel capacity to insure returning against adverse winds. Fighters were accustomed to attack under any and all conditions requiring the best possible performance in speed and climb. Thus, as a result of military necessities, fine desirable qualifications of an airplane were improved: speed, reliability, great strength for a minimum of weight, low gross weight, and high-powered engines.

And that is the way the tide of battle turned in the air during the first war. It swung like a pendulum, from side to side. First Garros had the advantage with his machine gun and deflector that enabled him to fire through the propeller arc. Then the Germans improved upon his invention by synchronizing the machine guns to the propeller, and their early aces, Oswald Boelcke, the "Red Baron's" mentor, and Max Immelmann, ranged the skies over the Western Front in their Fokker *Eindekkers* practically unopposed. The Allies countered with aircraft that circumvented the problem of synchronizing the machine gun to the prop. The British entered the lists with the D.H. 2, a pusher-type aircraft with the motor and prop behind the pilot, leaving him free to fire forward. The French brought out the trim "V" strut Nieuport 11 with the machine gun mounted on the top wing so that it would fire above the propeller arc. The Model 11 was affectionately called "Bébé" by the *Armée de l'Air* and the American fliers in the *Lafayette Escadrille*. It was soon superseded by the more attractive and more powerful little Nieuport 17. These great scouts succeeded in neutralizing the "Fokker Scourge," but they in turn were eclipsed by the sleek, streamlined German series of fine Albatros fighters. Upon graduating from the slower two-seater observation planes he flew at the start of his flying career, the "Red Baron" was assigned an Albatros, which he later had painted red all over, giving rise to his nickname.

The Albatroses ruled the skies until they were bested by the British S.E. 5's and Sopwith Camels, and the French SPAD VII's and XIII's. In turn, these great flying craft were matched by the German Fokker D VII's and Fokker Triplanes.

There is no question about the fact that war is truly as General Sherman described it, but it is also true that "it is an ill wind that blows no good." Four years of war created an aviation industry in all of the principal nations of the world, trained many thousands of fliers and mechanics, caught the attention of the public, called upon the wits and ingenuity of engineers and scientists, and developed from the frail crates of 1914 that could barely move at 60 mph the relatively superior, sturdier Fokker D VII's and SPAD XIII's of 1918 that moved along in level flight at more than twice that speed. In short, the war gave the airplane its start as a principal means of transportation (as World War II gave rise to the jet, space travel, and atomic energy) and probably accelerated the process threefold or more.

By all odds, the most spectacular feature of aerial warfare was the dogfighting, in which individual pilots or groups from both sides engaged in a kind of gladiatorial combat that carried them all over the sky. It so gripped the imagination of Americans that it gave rise to a new field of combat literature. But perhaps of more significance militarily were the development of strategic bombing, aerial mapping and photography, ground-support tactics, anti-submarine patroling, tactical naval aviation, and antiaircraft artillery.

Illustrated History of World War I in the Air is the pictorial story of the colorful battles fought in the sky during the dramatic years of 1914–18. It is the story of those gallant men and their magnificent flying machines who went aloft daily to meet their adversaries in mortal combat, in the clear blue sky. Like the knights of the Middle Ages they sallied forth, in their frail craft, to do battle.

The pages that follow are replete with the adventures of the great aces—French, British, Canadian, American, Belgian, Russian, Italian, and German; names like René Fonck, Georges Guynemer, Charles Nungesser, James McCudden, Billy Bishop, Eddie Rickenbacker, Charles J. Biddle, George A. Vaughn, Frank Luke, Willy Coppens, Ivan Kazakoff, Francesco Barraca, Baron Manfred von Richthofen, Ernst Udet, and many more.

These heroes flashed across the sky strapped in the cockpits of their Farmans, Taubes, Caudrons, Voisins, De Havillands, Nieuports, Spads, Fokkers, Albatroses, S.E.5's, Sopwith Camels, and other scout-fighters, reconnaissance, and bomber aircraft.

This book tells the dramatic, colorful story of high adventure in word and exciting art. It takes you from the primitive beginning in 1914, when opposing pilots, bent on reconnaissance missions in unarmed aircraft, peacefully waved to each other as they passed in the air, through the development of the machine gun that was synchronized to fire between the whirling propeller blades, and the improvment of the fighter plane and tactics leading to mass dogfights between Allied Spads, Sopwith Camels, and S.E.5's on one side, and German Fokkers and Albatroses on the other.

This was aerial combat in 1918!

Illustrated History of World War I in The Air

"The Birth of Powered Winged Flight" by Charles H. Hubbell

THE PIONEERS

The Birth of Powered Winged Flight

BARELY SIXTY-FIVE years ago, the miracle of powered winged flight took place. Hardly spectacular by today's standards, Orville Wright's first flight covered some 120 feet—considerably shorter even than the 140-foot wingspan of the giant German World War I bombers, the Staaken R planes (see page 87), built only twelve years later to bomb London.

Moreover, the flight lasted barely twelve seconds, for an average speed of ten feet per second. By comparison, one of today's jet fighters traveling at Mach 2, or approximately 14,000 miles per hour, would cover more than 20,000 feet per second.

That first flight over the dunes of Kitty Hawk, North Carolina, by the two bicycle manufacturers of Dayton, Ohio, was the portent of things to come—the Age of Flight.

"The U.S. Army Sprouts Wings" by Charles H. Hubbell

© 1957 TRW

The U.S. Army Sprouts Wings

THE WRIGHT brothers bid won the first U.S. Army airplane contract on February 10, 1908. The specifications stipulated that the aircraft had to carry two men at a minimum of 40 mph for a one-hour flight.

That same year the Wrights delivered their first model to Fort Meyer, just across the Potomac River from Washington, D.C., Orville Wright made the first test flight on September 3, and six days later he broke all endurance records by flying for fifty-seven minutes and twenty-five seconds, and making fifty-seven trips around the field at an altitude of over 100 feet. That same day Lt. Frank P. Lahm became the first Army passenger carried in the "Wright Flier" during the tests at Ft. Meyer.

Tragedy struck on September 17, when the plane crashed, killing Lt. Thomas E. Selfridge and injuring Orville Wright. This was the world's first fatal airplane crash.

The Wright brothers in the second test aircraft, on October 27, satisfied part of the contract specifications when Orville, with Lt. Lahm as passenger, established a new endurance record of one hour, twelve minutes and two seconds. Three days later, in another test, the aircraft completed a ten-mile cross-country flight over a stipulated course at a speed of 42.6 mph.

The plane was officially accepted on August 2, 1909.

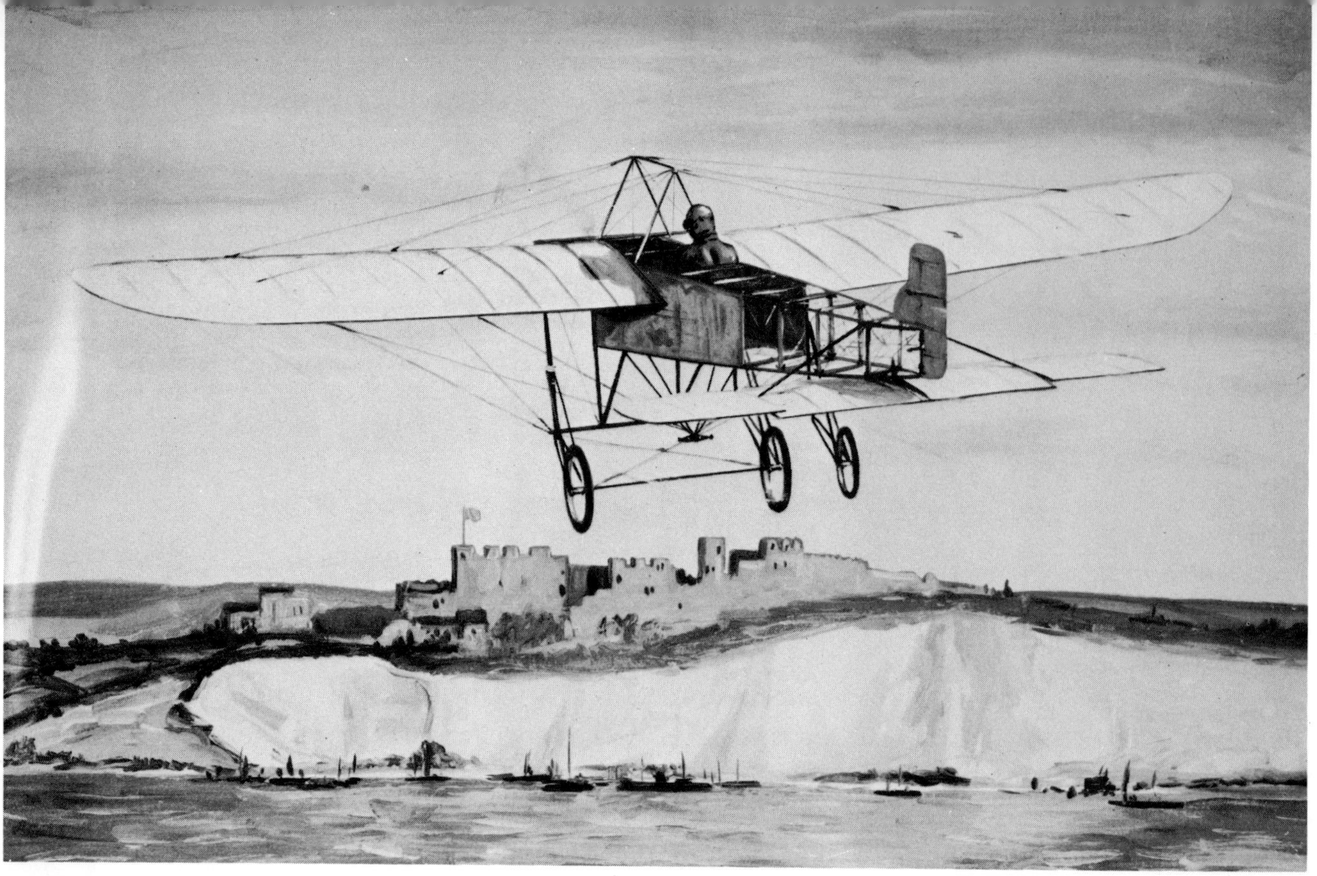

"First Over the Channel" by Charles H. Hubbell

© 1941 Thompson Products, Inc.

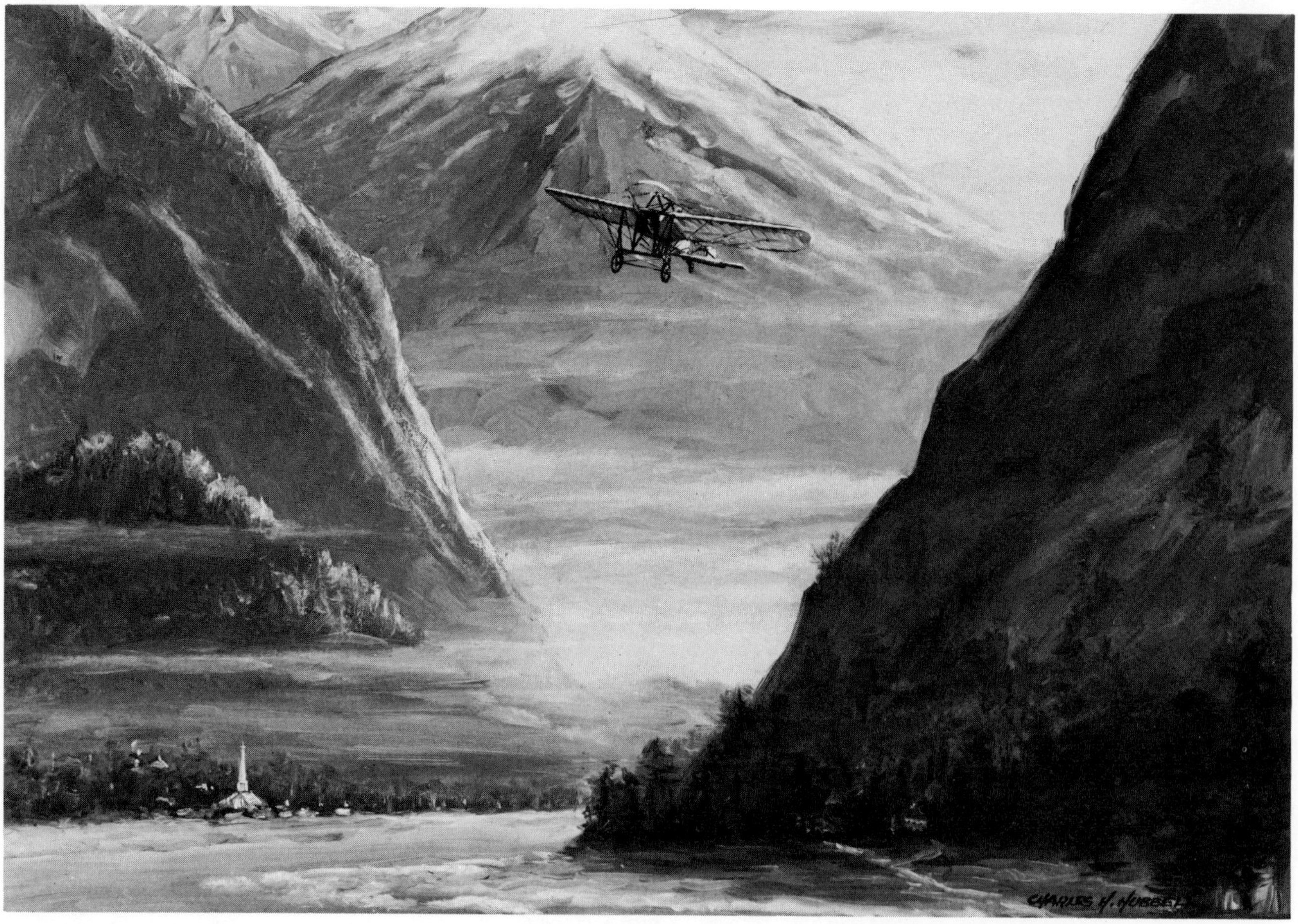

"A Blériot Flies the Alps" by Charles H. Hubbell

© 1967 TRW

First Over the Channel

ON JULY 25, 1909, the Frenchman Louis Blériot, in the aircraft he designed and built, became the first to fly across the English Channel. By doing so he won the £1,000 prize offered by the London *Daily Mail.*

Although he was deathly sick with an infected foot, the result of a gasoline explosion, Blériot was forced into making the flight at the time he did. He had been hobbling around on crutches for days. However, shortly before his flight another Frenchman, Hubert Latham, made the attempt, only to be forced down into the Channel by a faulty motor, after covering about seven miles. He was rescued by a French naval vessel ordered to follow his course as a safety measure.

Blériot knew that Latham would try again, and soon.

So at four o'clock in the morning, Louis Blériot mounted his monoplane and flew from Les Barrages, France, to Dover, England.

The Blériot XI proved to be a superior flying machine and distinguished itself in many events in the years preceding the war.

The conquest of the Alps was among its numerous accomplishments.

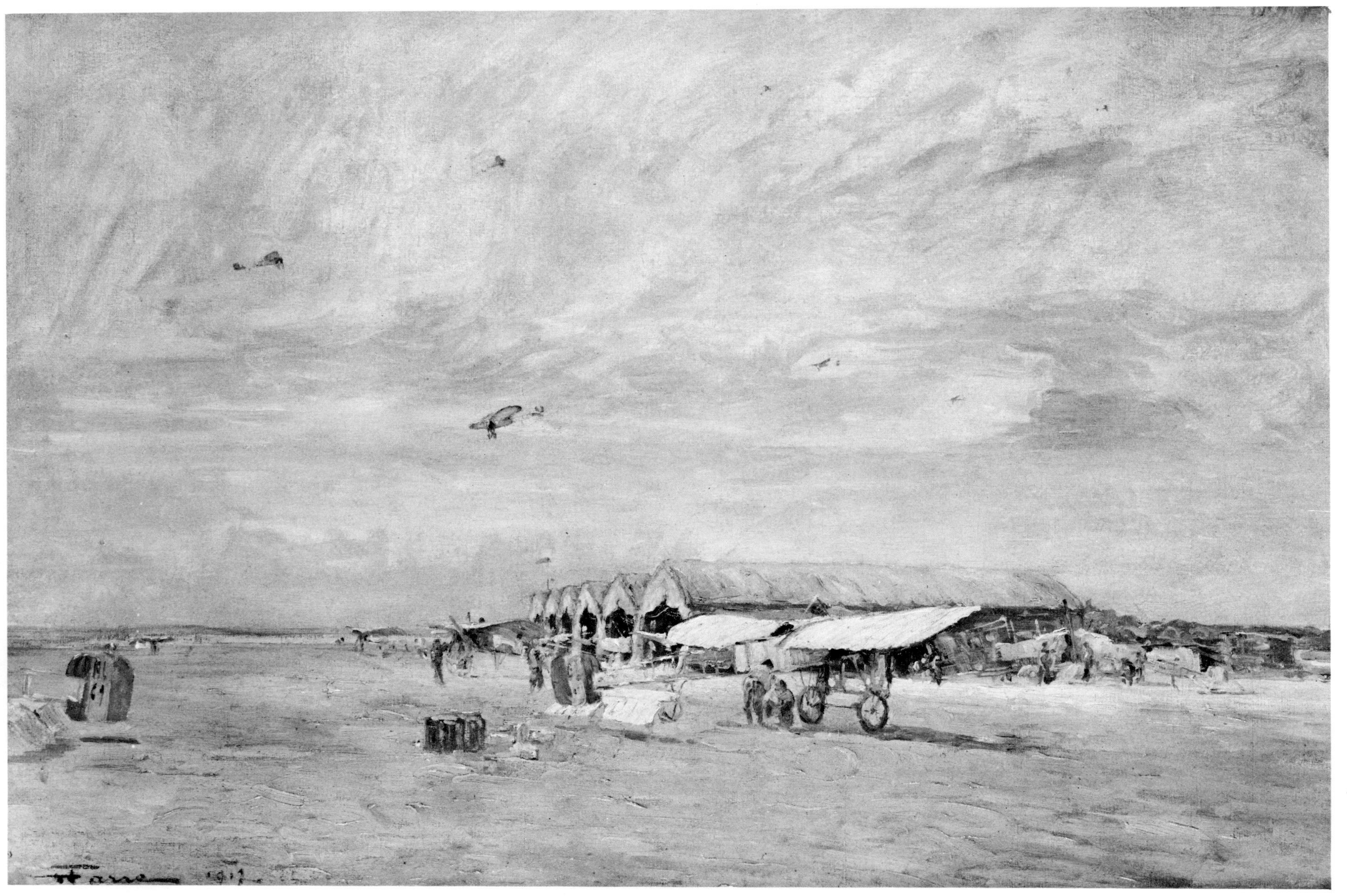

"A 10-Year-Old Goes to War" by Henry Farré
USAF Art Collection

THE FIGHTERS

A 10-Year-Old Goes to War

WHEN WAR broke out in August 1914, the airplane was little more than ten years old. The Blériot XI type, in which its namesake first negotiated the English Channel successfully, was just five years of age. It had already been to war in 1911 with the Italian forces in North Africa.

At the outbreak of World War I, the British Royal Flying Corps (RFC) took twenty-three Blériot XI's across to France with its expeditionary force, and they served as reconnaissance aircraft with six RFC squadrons. The French *Service de l'Aviation* similarly furnished models of this aircraft to some eight of their *escadrilles*, and the Italians, who had already committed the Blériot in an earlier fracas, went into action with six squadrons armed with the Blériot XI.

The military model of 1914 differed from its historic 1909 predecessor principally in that it carried a more powerful motor. Although the single-seater variety had only fifteen more horsepower than the original 35-hp Anzani motor, the two-seater jobs had double the original power. Three-seater models with 140-hp Gnôme engines had twice as much power.

Although their immediate successors were not much more advanced technologically, the box kitelike Blériots were truly ancient. They were, however, pioneers and forerunners of the great aircraft that would appear on the scene in the following two to four years.

"The Start of Aerial Warfare" by Charles F. Hubbell

The Start of Aerial Warfare

THE AIRPLANE, or *aeroplane* as it was then called and still is in Great Britain, was not looked upon as an instrument of destruction, but rather as a "scout." Even at the end of the war such relatively high performance fighters as the Sopwith Camel and S.E.5 were officially designated scouts. These early aircraft were much like the scouts who preceded the troops during the Indian wars of the latter half of the nineteenth century in the U.S. In the beginning of the First World War, cavalry served as the eyes of their respective armies and roamed the countryside to scout out the enemy and report on his movements. The airplane, because of the altitude it was able to attain and its relative freedom of movement without harassment from the enemy, proved to be the best scout of all.

And indeed their flights were peaceful. Pilots and observers of the opposing sides waved and smiled at each other, in some sort of camaraderie of the sky, as they passed in the air, each bent on scouting out the other side's positions. Their aircraft were completely unarmed, while on the battlefield below their earth-bound fellows, like two giant juggernauts, locked horns and fought with fire and steel and died for only inches of ground.

The peaceful air was not to remain calm and quiet for too long, however. History has not recorded who the first pilot was to attack his opponent in the air, but the sequence of events most probably went something like this—a flier whose friendly smile or greeting was answered by a thumbed nose or similar gesture of disdain carried bricks or other missiles aloft with him on his next flight. These he gleefully dropped on the first unsuspecting opponent who happened along. Such exchanges continued as fliers attempted to best each other. Soon they were carrying rifles and pistols into the air, and traded shots.

"A Machine Gun Fired Through the Propeller Arc Claims Its First Air-to-Air Victim" by Charles F. Hubbell

A Machine Gun Fired Through the Propeller Arc Claims Its First Air-to-Air Victim

ROLAND GARROS, who had been a famous French stunt flier before the war, had a machine gun mounted on the fuselage of his Morane-Saulnier N, in front of his cockpit. It was set up to fire forward, and all he had to do was to point his plane at an adversary and squeeze the trigger. The only "fly in the ointment" was that his machine's wooden propeller stood between him and the enemy aircraft and would undoubtedly be shot off, bringing Garros and his plane crashing to their end on the earth below. The Frenchman remedied this situation by having steel plates attached to the propeller blades at machine gun level. Thus those bullets that would have sheared off his prop were deflected, and the others got through to wreak havoc among the German flying machines.

Garros' development was an instant success. There was really nothing in the Kaiser's air service to oppose him. However, ill fortune in the form of a forced landing behind enemy lines placed him and his aircraft in German hands. In true chivalric fashion they wined and dined their captive and set their engineers to studying his invention.

"Slingshot Against a Giant" by Charles H. Hubbell

Slingshot Against a Giant

STRAPPED INTO the cockpit of his tiny Morane-Saulnier scout (the painting shows an MS N, but it was actually an MS L Parasol), Lt. R.A.J. Warneford of the British Royal Naval Air Service was flying toward Ostend. It was his first night flight, and his mission was to bomb the Zeppelin sheds at Evere. Suddenly he spotted a giant cigar-shaped object sailing through the clouds. Coming in closer for a better look, he made out the large black Maltese crosses of the Imperial German Air Service on the sides of the behemoth. And to make identification more positive, it opened up on him with its machine guns.

It was the LZ 37, a German Zeppelin, 521 feet long, kept aloft by 935,000 cubic feet of dangerously inflammable hydrogen, and armed with four machine guns.

Warneford's single-seater Morane-Saulnier Parasol L carried only a few bombs and a carbine. The "Zep" was still firing at him as they dumped ballast and rapidly bolted higher into the air.

He struggled to gain altitude, still following the big gas bag. Early into the morning, Warneford relentlessly tracked the enemy Zeppelin. His break finally came when, for some strange reason, the Zep nosed down, decreasing its altitude. Warneford pushed his little Morane up until he was above the giant, and he released his bombs.

It seemed like an eternity, but suddenly the air was rent with a tremendous explosion, and the big gas bag went down wrapped in flame. Warneford had been the first Allied flier to bring down a Zeppelin. The date was June 7, 1915.

A PRE-WAR fighter, the Morane-Saulnier L first appeared in 1913. It was called "Parasol" because the single wing was suspended over the fuselage like an umbrella held by struts and wire. The model L was first in a long line of Parasols designed by Morane-Saulnier.

This type aircraft was used by Lt. Warneford when he brought down the German dirigible and earned the Victoria Cross. It was also flown by Georges Guynemer when he gained his first victory.

Some authorities believe that it was the MS L Parasol rather than the mid-wing monoplane N model on which Garros had the Hotchkiss machine gun fitted and the steel deflectors attached to his propeller blades.

The Morane-Saulnier N

THE STREAMLINING of the Morane-Saulnier N put it way ahead of its time. It was in fact shown to be superior to the Fokker E III, which followed it.

In addition to serving in a number of French *escadrilles*, the MS N also was furnished to two British squadrons and to the Russians.

It was flown by French aces Jean Navarre, Roland Garros, and Adolphe Pegoud. Russian aces of the 19th Fighter Squadron also flew Morane-Saulnier N's, with a large white skull and crossbones on a black painted rudder, including Alexander Kazakov and Ivan Smirnoff. The British called it the "Bullet" because of its sleek lines (see p. 73).

Kazakov Scores for Russia

LIKE HIS British and German contemporaries, Billy Bishop and Manfred von Richthofen, Staff-Captain Alexander Alexandrovich Kazakov had been a cavalry officer when the war began, but he too forsook the saddle for the cockpit.

By early 1915, Kazakov was in combat and, on March 18, he brought down his first enemy aircraft. His victory, however, was an unorthodox one. Kazakov came up with a real brainstorm. He had an anchor on a cable attached to a reel rigged to the bottom of his Morane-Saulnier N. Unfortunately, the cable jammed in the reel during his first attempt to use it. With the enemy observer firing on him, Kazakov dived on the Albatros two-seater and rammed him with his wheels.

Kazakov went on to become Russia's ace-of-aces. He commanded Fighter Group 1 which was made up of four fighter squadrons, including the "Death or Glory" 19th. By the end of the war he was credited with seventeen victories, although he had destroyed a great many more. During the Russian Revolution he flew with the RAF.

Jack Leynnwood's painting shows Kazakov's fellow ace Ivan Smirnoff in action in an MS N (see p. 73).

The Eagle of Lille

OBERLEUTNANT* MAX Immelmann earned the nickname *Der Adler von Lille* (the Eagle of Lille) following his exploits in the Fokker *Eindekker*, newly armed with the synchronized Spandau machine gun. He was a contemporary of Oswald Boelcke's and his name is forever inscribed in the book of fighter pilot jargon for the tactic known as the "Immelmann Turn."

He was an early hero of the Imperial German Air Service and the first to score in the *Eindekker*. He was awarded the *Pour le Mérite* following his eighth victory.

Immelmann lost his life on June 18, 1916, when the observer in a British FE 2b pusher brought him down with a burst of fire (see p. 74).

* First Lieutenant.

The Fokker Scourge

THE BALANCE of power in the air war of 1914-18 swung like a pendulum. First one side had the advantage; then the other side would come up with an improvement that swayed the balance in their favor.

First the Allies had the advantage with Garros' device, and then Fokker's *Eindekker*-synchronized Spandau machine gun weapon system stole the lead. The great advantage of the *Eindekker*-Spandau team, and its devastating destructive power against relatively weaker aircraft, earned it the awesome title of the "Fokker Scourge." As a corollary the British also called their own inferior aircraft, "Fokker Fodder."

The Fokker *Eindekker* was not a great aircraft but its synchronized machine gun made it a formidable foe (see p. 75).

"Anthony Fokker Improves on Garros' Invention" by Charles H. Hubbell

Anthony Fokker Improves on Garros' Invention

THE URGENT task of perfecting a system of firing through the arc of the whirling propeller was assigned to Anthony Fokker. In less than forty-eight hours the Dutch aeronautical engineer and manufacturer of that great line of German fighter planes, improved considerably on Garros' invention.

Fokker *Eindekkers,* armed with synchronized Spandau machine guns, roamed the skies virtually unopposed. Piloted by such German aces as Max Immelmann and Oswald Boelke they wreaked havoc among the unsuspecting British and French. But as things went in that first war in the air, it was not long before the Allies too had their synchronized gun developed by Georges Constantinesco.

In his recently published book *Fighting Airman—The Way of the Eagle,* Major Charles J. Biddle, scion of the Philadelphia Biddles and a leading U.S. World War I ace, described the principle of the synchronized machine gun.

> There is no mystery about a machine gun firing through a propeller without hitting the blades. Nearly everyone understands the principle by which the valves of a gasoline motor are timed so as to open and close at a given point in the revolution of the engine. In the same way a machine gun may be timed to shoot. On the end of the cam shaft of the motor is placed an additional cam. Next to this is a rod connected with the breech block of the gun. When the gun is not being fired the rod is held away from the cam by a spring. Pressing the trigger brings the two into contact, and each time the cam revolves it strikes the rod which in turn trips the hammer of the gun and causes it to fire. The cam is regulated so that it comes in contact with the rod just as each blade has passed the muzzle of the gun which can therefore fire at this time only. The engine revolves at least 1,000 turns per minute and as there are two chances for the gun to fire for each revolution, this would allow the gun to fire 2,000 shots per minute. The rate of fire of a machine gun varies from about 400 to 1,000 shots per minute according to the type of gun and the way in which it is rigged. The gun therefore has many more opportunities to fire between the blades of the propeller than its rate of fire will permit it to make use of. Consequently, the gun can work at full speed regardless of ordinary variations in the number of revolutions of the engine.

The Eastern Central Power

WITH THE introduction of the British DH 2, other pusher-type aircraft, and the French Nieuports, the legend of the invincibility of the Fokker *Eindekkers* began to fade rapidly. The death of Immelmann in June of 1916 was probably the death knell of the "Fokker Scourge."

Eindekkers continued to serve on the Eastern Front, however. They remained in service in Palestine, Mesopotamia, and Turkey until the end of that year.

The E III's shown in the illustration bear the black square insignia of Turkey (see p. 75).

England's Answer to the "Fokker Scourge"

AS THE SCORE of the Fokker *Eindekkers* continued to mount, British aircraft designers and engineers worked feverishly to come up with a fighter that could at least meet that enemy scout on equal terms.

The answer was the DH 2, a single-seater pusher type aircraft designed by Geoffrey de Havilland of Airco (Aircraft Manufacturing Co.). The DH 2 was an odd-looking crate. It had an extremely short fuselage containing the cockpit, motor and machine gun. The pilot sat forward of the motor and propeller with the machine gun mounted in front of him having a free field of fire. Two booms attached to the wings extended to the rear and supported the rudder and tail control surfaces (see p. 77).

This strange flying machine proved to be the master of the *Eindekker.* The prototype appeared in mid-1915 but the first production models were not delivered until January of the following year. That was the beginning of the end for the Fokker E III.

PRIOR TO January 1916, no squadrons had been organized specifically for the purpose of destroying enemy aircraft. First of these fighter units was No. 24 Squadron RFC.

Armed with the new De Havilland 2 single-seater scout, No. 24 Squadron landed in France on February 7, 1916. They were under the command of Major Lanoe G. Hawker, V.C. who had already earned the reputation of being a great fighter pilot.

Hawker, although quiet and shy, was an aggressive fighter pilot. He was a graduate of the Royal Military College and was one of the first to be trained as a pilot. By the time he took command of No. 24 Squadron he had been flying in combat for a year-and-a-quarter, since the beginning of the war. He had already earned the Distinguished Service Order, the Victoria Cross, and had attained the rank of Major. Although the record officially credited Hawker with nine victories, a number of experts and reliable air historians claim he shot down between thirty and fifty-five aircraft before the British kept such records.

Under Major Hawker's leadership, No. 24 Squadron became a prime fighting force that played a great part in destroying the *Eindekker* nemesis.

Hawker himself, in an unforgettable battle, became the eleventh victim of the "Red Baron." He was shot down and killed on November 23, 1916.

"De Havilland 2" by Gene Thomas
© *Renwal Products Inc.*

"Flying Fury—Maj. James T. B. McCudden"
by Clyde A. Risley

Flying Fury

On July 9, 1918, engine failure accomplished what hundreds of the enemy, their fighter planes, and their antiaircraft guns had failed to do.

Major James Thomas Byford McCudden, V.C., D.S.O. & Bar, M.C. & Bar, M.M., *Croix de Guerre,* the British air services' most decorated member, veteran of five years in the Royal Flying Corps (R.F.C.) and the Royal Air Force (R.A.F.), victor in fifty-seven dramatic battles in the air, crashed to his death in his S.E.5a. He was twenty-two years old.

Jim McCudden was the fourth-ranking ace on the unofficial British Empire list of the Great War, 1914-18. But for his untimely death he might well have bettered his score and climbed up a few rungs on the list. He was a keen, daring, yet resourceful air fighter.

He began his military career as a bugler in the Royal Engineers in 1910. Three years later he transferred to the fledgling R.F.C. where he served as a mechanic. Shortly after the outbreak of war, his squadron shipped to France. McCudden rose through the enlisted ranks to the grade of Flight Sergeant. He was anxious to fly and occasionally went aloft as an observer. Unofficially he even got in some piloting time on a Morane Parasol.

McCudden fought his first air battle "in the back seat," as an observer, on December 19, 1915, and the following month he returned to England for pilot training.

In six months he was back at the front, flying two-seater reconnaissance and escort missions. But the following month, on August 3, 1916, he was assigned to No. 29 Squadron where he flew D.H.2's on scout and fighter patrols. One month later, on September 6, he scored his first victory.

McCudden received the King's Commission as a Second Lieutenant in January 1917. During the next year-and-a-half, up to his accidental death, McCudden ran up a fantastic number of victories as fifty-seven German planes withered before his guns.

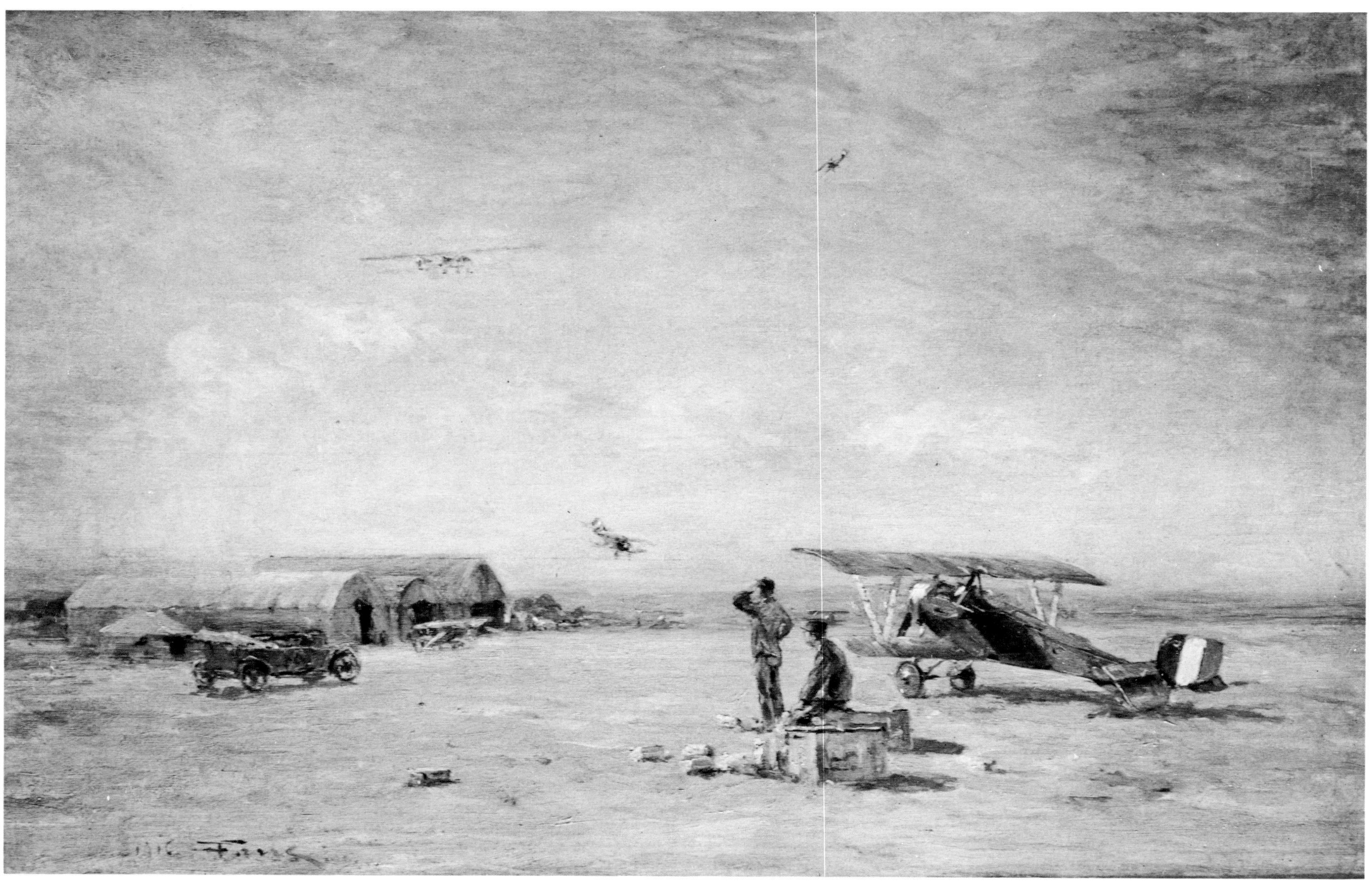

"France's Answer to the 'Fokker Scourge'" by Henry Farré
USAF Art Collection

V France's Answer to the "Fokker Scourge"

DESIGNED ORIGINALLY as a racing plane to compete in the Gordon Bennett race of 1914, the Nieuport 11 was quickly recruited for military service at the outbreak of war.

It was a tiny machine with an extremely narrow lower wing. Its small size won it the affectionate sobriquet of *Bébé* or "Baby." The Nieuport 11 was armed with a single Lewis gun mounted in the center of the upper wing. It fired forward above the propeller arc.

Most of the French aces sharpened their fighting teeth in the *Bébé* and it was also flown by Americans in the *Escadrille Lafayette.* Nieuport 11's of the British RNAS and RFC flew alongside the DH 2's and FE 2b's and played a part in neutralizing the "Fokker Scourge."

Many Nieuport 11's were manufactured in Italy by Macchi. These served with the Italian Air Force. Belgium, Russia, and the Netherlands also used the little fighter.

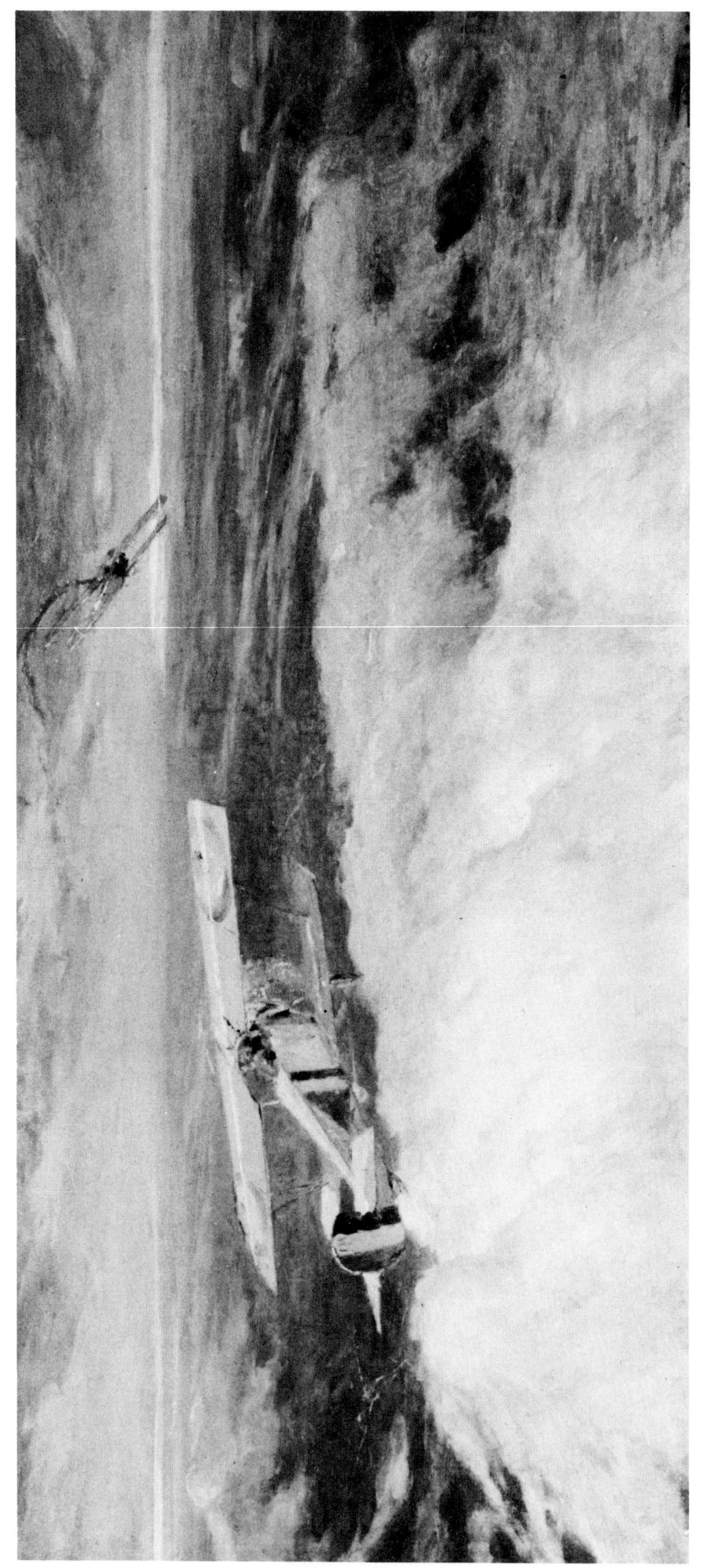

"Airplane Duel Over the Verdun Front" by Henry Farré
USAF Art Collection

First Double for France

LT. JEAN NAVARRE had earned his wings as a military pilot before the start of the war. He flew observation aircraft before they were armed and even went aloft after a German Zeppelin with a kitchen knife as his only weapon.

Navarre is credited with a number of "firsts." He was France's first ace to achieve fame. Earlier in his career he and his observer forced down intact an enemy Aviatik with only three bullets fired from a rifle. In the dramatic scene depicted here by Joe Phelan, Navarre, in his red Nieuport *Bébé,* is dispatching an Albatros two-seater over Verdun, following his repeat performance of forcing down an enemy machine intact on an earlier patrol that day (February 26, 1916), the first double for France (see p. 76).

Airplane Duel Over the Verdun Front

IN THIS battle above the clouds the Nieuport 11 has already given the *coup de grâce* to the German machine. Although it is trailing smoke, the French pilot will follow his adversary down to make sure that it is not a ruse and that the enemy will not try to make a run for it.

Had there been other enemy aircraft in the vicinity the Frenchman could not have afforded the luxury of making certain of his victory.

"Destruction of Observation Balloons by Incendiary Rockets" by Charles H. Hubbell

Destruction of Observation Balloons by Incendiary Rockets

For all intents and purposes the Nieuport 16 was exactly the same as the model 11 except for a few minor differences and a more powerful motor. Otherwise the outside dimensions and appearance of both machines were precisely the same.

The *Bébé* was powered by an 80-hp Gnôme rotary engine while the 16 had a 110-hp-Le Rhône. Both were mounted in a horseshoe-shaped cowling. The later model also had a synchronized Vickers machine gun mounted on the fuselage in front of the pilot which replaced the "Baby's" Lewis gun fastened to the top of the upper wing. (By the time the Nieuport 16 appeared on the scene the Germans had their synchronized Spandau machine gun and the Allies had the interrupter gear perfected by Constantinesco.)

The biggest difference between the two models, however, was the eight Le Prieur rockets that could be fitted to the V-struts of the Nieuport 16, four to each set of interplane struts. These rockets were fired electrically by the pilot from the cockpit.

The Le Prieur rockets were used with some success in attacking enemy observation balloons.

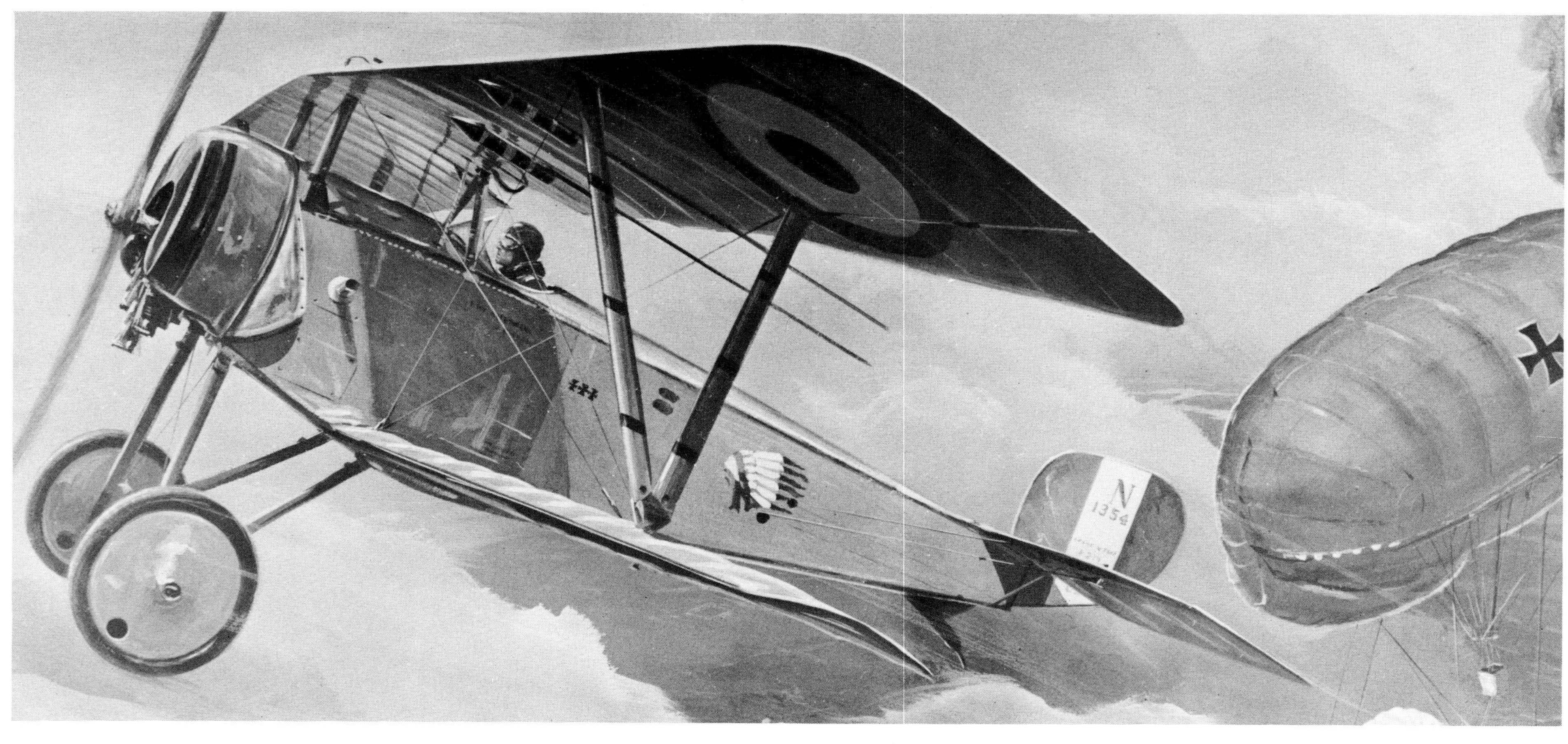

"First Air-to-Air Rockets"

First Air-to-Air Rockets

THE "SIDEWINDER" air-to-air missiles used successfully by pilots of our Phantom jets against MIG 21's in Vietnam are direct descendants of the Le Prieur rockets of 1916. Although the Chinese had used rockets in warfare centuries before, they had been surface-to-surface rockets. The Le Prieur rockets were the first to be employed on an air-to-air mission.

"Destruction of Observation Balloons" by Henry Farré
USAF Art Collection

"The Belgian Balloon Buster—
Lt. Willy Coppens" by Clyde A. Risley

The Belgian Balloon Buster—
Lieutenant Willy Coppens

VERY MUCH alive and kicking today is the peppery little Baron Coppens de Houthulst. He lives in the tiny seacoast town of La Panne in his native Belgium. It is the same town near which he fought his last air battle a few weeks before the close of World War I and where he recuperated after losing a leg as a result of that encounter.

Will Coppens became his country's ace-of-aces with a total of thirty-four confirmed victories. Of this total, very few were winged aircraft. In the main they were observation balloons that fell before his flaming guns.

Although Coppens flew a Nieuport at first, most of his victories were gained in the Hanriot HD 1. Other nations too had their "Balloon Busters," men who delighted in setting a torch to the giant gas bags. The French Air Service boasted of Michel Coiffard, who like Coppens had thirty-four victories, twenty-eight of which were *drachens*. The U.S. too, had its Arizona cowboy, Lt. Frank Luke, Jr.

Luke was unruly, a braggart, and undisciplined, but he was a superior fighter pilot. In a period of only nine days, which included less than thirty hours of flying time, he accounted for nineteen enemy aircraft destroyed. Of this total, fifteen were balloons. On his last flight he crash landed behind enemy lines and rather than surrender fought it out against a squad of German infantry with only a Colt .45 automatic in his hand, until he was killed.

"Aeroplanes Approaching Over Hangars, 1917" by Henry Farré

Aeroplanes Approaching Over Hangars

From the late summer of 1915 until the appearance of production models of the Spad VII in the fall of 1916, the Nieuports made up the bulk of the French fighter or scout forces. In fact, Nieuport fighters remained in French *escadrilles* until the summer of 1917 and were preferred by some of the French aces, including Nungesser, to the more powerful Spad.

The Nieuport line designed by Gustave Delage began with the two-seater Nieuport 10 which was furnished to the squadrons during the summer of 1915. It was underpowered for a two-seater and was often flown as a single-seater. *Capitaine* Brocard, of later "Stork" fame, brought down an enemy machine with a pistol early in July of that year, while flying it as a single-seater. A larger, more powerful Model 12 was built but the first really great one was the Nieuport 11. A single-seater, it was supplied to the *escadrilles de chasse*, the RNAS, the RFC and together with the DH 2 succeeded in neutralizing the threat of the Fokker *Eindekkers*. The best of Delage's designs, however, was the trim Nieuport 17 which ruled the skies from March 1916 until the appearance of the German Albatros scouts. The 17 was succeeded by the more powerful and better streamlined models 24 and 27, but they were no match for the Spad VII's and XIII's which replaced them.

Last of the wartime Nieuports was the model 28 supplied to newly arriving American squadrons. It met with disfavor because of the weakness of its wing structure and was dropped in favor of the Spad XIII.

"An Unlikely Hero—Capt. Georges Guynemer" by Henry Farré

USAF Art Collection

An Unlikely Hero–Captain Georges Guynemer

On September 11, 1917, a young man who had become a legend in his own time flew off "into the blue" never to return.

Georges Guynemer was only a boy, like many of his counterparts in the British, German, and American air services. His contemporaries were the great English Captain Albert Ball, who earned the Victoria Cross and scored forty-four victories before he himself was shot down, and the indomitable enemy ace Werner Voss who was awarded his country's highest honor for valor—the *Pour le Mérite*—while he was still in his teens. All three of these young heroes were killed in action.

But even despite his extreme youth Guynemer was still an unlikely hero. He was frail of body and was a consumptive. At a time when physical examinations and physical requirements for flight training were practically nil by today's rigorous standards, it was still amazing that he made it. But he did make it and he went on to become a hero of France and, for a period of time, his nation's leading ace and champion.

At the time of his death, Guynemer was officially credited with fifty-four victories and by the end of the war he ranked second on the French list of aces. His death was avenged by his fellow "Stork" and successor, René Fonck.

"Guynemer and the 'Storks'" by Jack Leynnwood

√ Guynemer and the "Storks"

WHILE THE British did not recognize the ace system and shied away from publicizing the scores or exploits of their fighter pilots, the French, on the other hand, fostered and encouraged it.

The cream of the French fighter aces were gathered into the Stork Group consisting of four squadrons. Any pilot showing promise in other scout or two-seater squadrons was usually assigned to the Storks. It was the dream and ambition of every little French boy to grow up to be a member of the Storks, and of every neophyte pilot to be found worthy of wearing the stork emblem on his uniform tunic and to have the stork insignia painted on the sides of his plane.

Each of the four Stork squadrons used the stork for its insignia, but each stork was in a different position or attitude of flight. *Escadrille* 3's stork's wings were down, No. 26's were at its side, No. 103's wings were up and *Escadrille* 73's stork was in a turning position.

At the outset Georges Guynemer was not a promising fighter pilot. However, he was assigned to *Escadrille* No. 3 on June 8, 1915 before the Storks had actually been organized. At the time they were flying Morane-Saulniers. Later these squadrons were equipped with Nieuports and then with Spads.

Jack Leynnwood's painting shows Guynemer in his Nieuport 17 with the Stork insignia rampant.

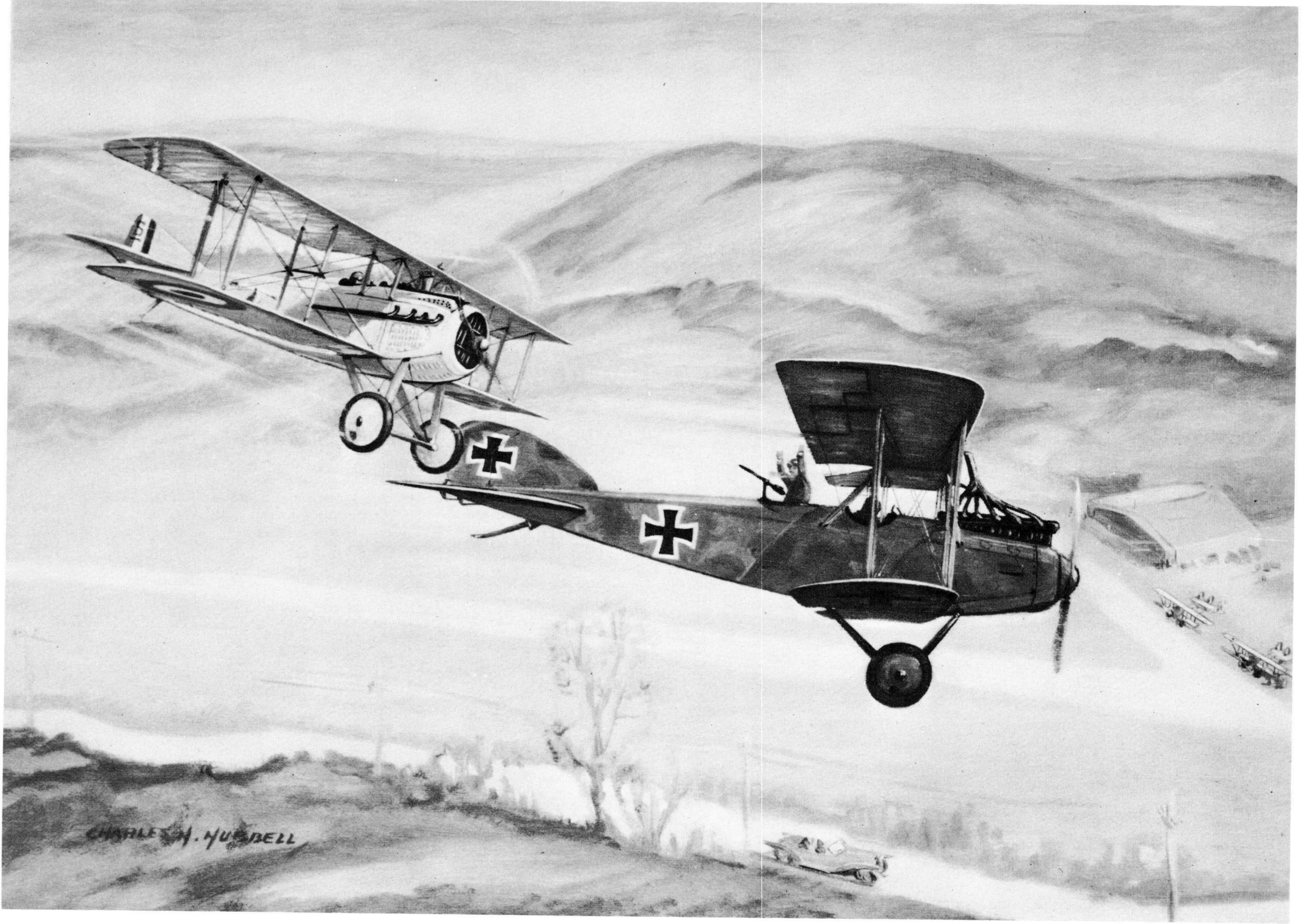

"Guynemer's Ruse" by Charles H. Hubbell

Guynemer's Ruse

Georges Guynemer was a living legend in France and every schoolboy knew his name, worshipped him as a hero, and avidly followed his exploits. Not only was he a hero to the civilian, the layman, and the *Poilu* (infantryman) in the trenches, he was a hero to his fellow Storks as well. Even this group of top-notch, battle-hardened fighter pilots, studded with aces and heroes, regarded Guynemer as "something else." They too looked up to him as an idol.

In his book *Ace of Aces*, René Fonck describes "bull sessions," following the death of Guynemer, where Storks tell of their exciting battles and feats in the air (using their hands as substitutes for planes in traditional fighter pilot manner), only to hear the response, "Guynemer would have done more," from fellow fighter aces.

The scene on the opposite page, "Guynemer's Ruse" by Charles H. Hubbell, colorfully shows one of the hero's dramatic exploits.

Guynemer, using raw courage instead of bullets, forced an Albatros C III to land at a French aerodrome. His Vickers machine gun had jammed and was completely inoperative.

See page 77 where Guynemer, still flying his Spad VII which he called "*Vieux Charles,*" or "Old Charlie," has just scored against two enemy Albatros single-seater scouts in A. Vimnèra's "A Double Victory for Guynemer."

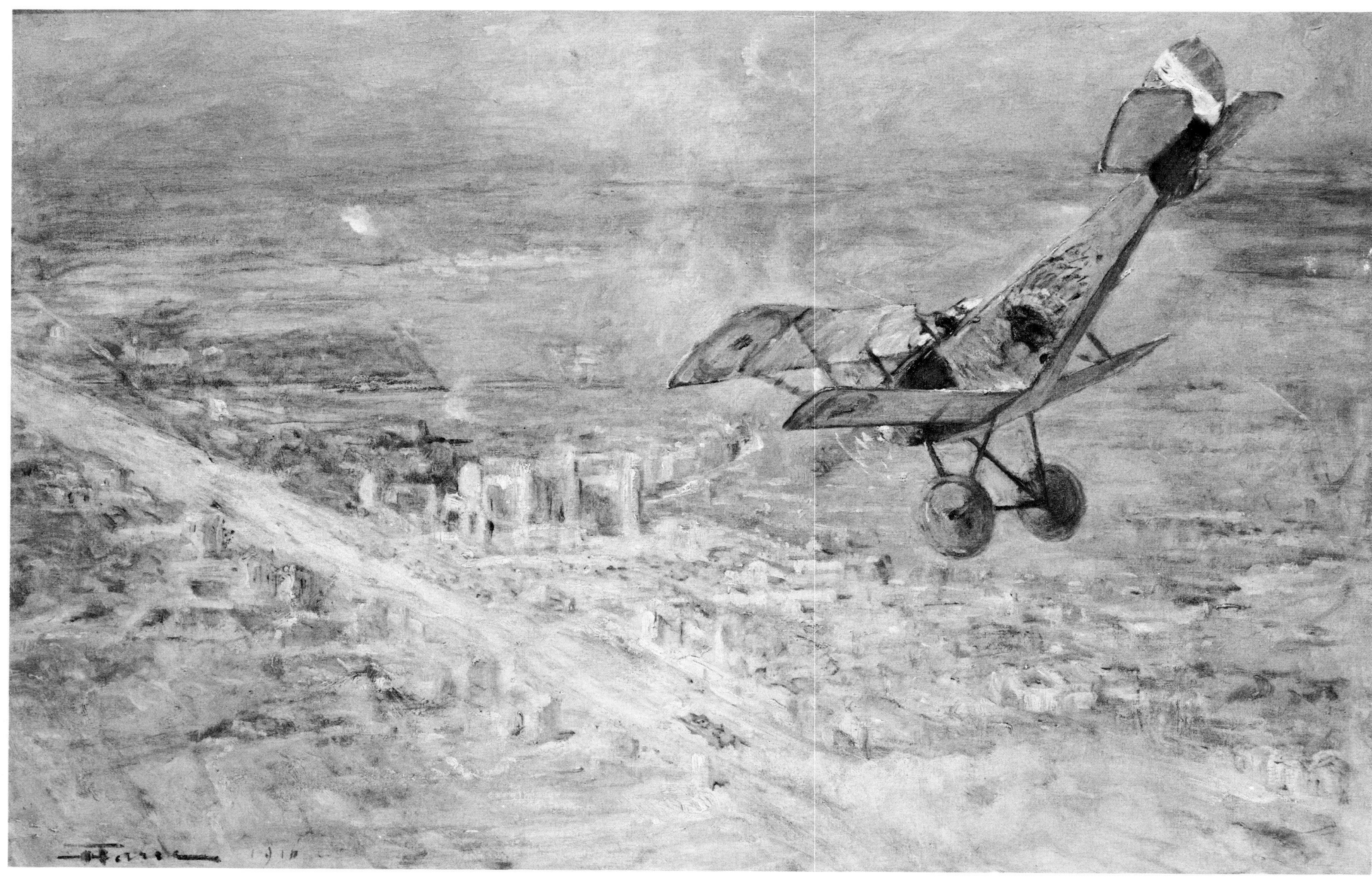

"Strafing a Town While Returning from Patrol" by Henry Farré
USAF Art Collection

Strafing a Town While Returning From Patrol

HENRY FARRÉ, the French combat artist, had been assigned the task of recording on canvas the activities of the air arm. To accomplish his mission he first flew with and painted the activities of bomber and reconnaissance squadrons, and then visited the Storks and the *Escadrille Lafayette*. He was very much impressed with these Americans, who came across the Atlantic to fight for France, and painted several scenes showing them in action in their Nieuports bearing their unique insignia—the head of a roaring American Indian.

The "dawn patrol" was a colorful and often dramatic mission. The planes took off before the sun rose over the horizon to seek out and destroy enemy observation planes or scouts whose mission was to destroy them. Sometimes the patrol encountered the enemy and a "dogfight ensued; at other times the flight would be uneventful. In either case, the pilots often expended their leftover ammunition on enemy troops in the trenches, enemy columns on the road, enemy trains, and enemy occupied towns.

"The 'Lafayette Escadrille'–Lt. Wm. Thaw" by Henry Farré

USAF Art Collection

The "Lafayette Escadrille"

ONE OF THE charter members of the *Lafayette Escadrille* was William Thaw. Along with Norman Prince, Kiffin Rockwell, Raoul Lufbery, Jim McConnell, Bert Hall, and other Americans, Bill Thaw learned to fly, and fought under the French *Tricoleur* before the United States entered the war. They had transferred from the Foreign Legion and the Ambulance Service. Although commanded by French officers (Captain Thénault and Lt. de Laage de Meux), Thaw was the senior American in the squadron with the rank of Lieutenant. Lufbery was the highest scoring member of the *Escadrille* with seventeen confirmed victories.

After the U.S. declared war in April 1917, those survivors of the Lafayette Flying Corps who met U.S. standards and wanted to, were commissioned in the American Air Service. Some continued to fly with the French, others were assigned to the U.S. 103rd Aero Squadron (which became known as the *Lafayette Escadrille*), and some were sent to other new American squadrons to provide a seasoned nucleus with combat experience. Thaw went on to command the 103rd and the 3rd Pursuit Group; and Lufbery was assigned to the 94th "Hat in the Ring" Squadron.

Both Thaw and Lufbery were commissioned Majors. Thaw was later promoted to the rank of Lieutenant Colonel. Lufbery died in action, when he jumped from a flaming Nieuport 28.

"Ball Catches a Whale" by Joseph A. Phelan

from Heroes and Aeroplanes of the Great War 1914–1918 *pub. by Grosset & Dunlap, © 1966*

Ball Catches a Whale

THE BRITISH made little of the exploits and deeds of their fighter pilots and did not recognize the "Ace" designation for fear of diminishing the morale of their pilots in two-seater observation and bomber squadrons, whose missions were not as spectacular as those of the fighter pilots. However, one RFC ace got some of the recognition due him.

Captain Albert Ball, who died in action while still in his teens, had earned the Distinguished Service Order and two bars, the Military Cross, and the highest awards for valor of three nations—the British Victoria Cross, the French *Legion d'Honneur*, and the Russian Order of St. George. He flew in action from early 1916 until May 7, 1917, and amassed a victory score of forty-four enemy aircraft.

Although the Red Baron's younger brother, Lothar, claimed the victory over Ball that May 7th, his report stated it was a Sopwith Triplane he shot down, but Ball was flying an SE 5. It is believed that he was actually brought down by machine gunners in a church tower which Ball frequently passed at belfry level.

Earlier in his career, before he flew the Nieuport 17 and SE 5, Ball flew a single-seater Bristol Scout. Artist Joe Phelan captured Ball's encounter with a flight of LFG Roland C II's. Because of their resemblance to the large seagoing mammal, the Germans called them "*Whalfisch*" or "whale."

"Bishop of Canada" by Clyde A. Risley

" 'V-Strutter' vs. 'V-Strutter' " by Charles H. Hubbell

Bishop Of Canada

ALTHOUGH A Canadian, Billy Bishop's boyhood was very much like that of any American boy who grew up in the Midwest or plains states during the same period. The similarity between that area and the middle Canadian provinces is remarkably close. Like any youth of high spirit and with a good sense of humor, young Billy got into his share of trouble. As a cadet in the Royal Military College he ran afoul of authority there. But the war was on and he received the King's Commission as a Cavalry officer.

Once in France, Lieutenant Bishop found that he did not care too much for the mud or life in the cavalry. He looked to the sky and was inspired by the thought of flight in the clean free air. Before too long Bishop's transfer came through to the Royal Flying Corps (RFC). Unfortunately, his training gave little indication or promise of his future formidable ability as a fighter pilot. In fact, he succeeded in demolishing a couple of British aircraft rather than German ones, and was about to be "washed out" as a flyer. As always, however, the customary Bishop luck prevailed. The RFC sorely needed pilots and the colonel gave him one more chance. Needless to say, Bishop made it.

His dash and daring gave the Allies one of their top fighter aces who participated in more than 170 air battles and emerged with seventy-two confirmed victories to his credit.

His career did not end here, however. Billy Bishop served his country again in World War II as Marshal of the Royal Canadian Air Force (RCAF), and his son fought as a fighter pilot in one of its squadrons.

Billy Bishop is an all-time great, one of that fabulous contingent of First World War Canadian aces that included his close friend and postwar business partner, Billy Barker; Ray Collishaw, leader of the famed Naval Black Flight; and Roy Brown, credited with shooting down the "Red Baron."

THE GERMAN Albatros D III is said to have been a copy of the French Nieuport 17, which preceded it at the front. Actually the Albatros was a superior machine, having arrived on the scene practically a year later during that period of rapid technological advancement. In the action illustrated here it was the superior pilot who won.

William Avery Bishop maneuvered himself onto the tail of the enemy and tore off his upper wing with a burst from his Lewis gun and sent the German spinning, out of control, to the earth below.

"The Indestructible Frenchman" by Henry Farré

USAF Art Collection

The Indestructible Frenchman

DESPITE SEVENTEEN wounds and injuries from crashes and enemy action, Lt. Charles Nungesser survived the war only to lose his life nine years later—in 1927, while attempting to fly the Atlantic.

Although he spent a great deal of time in the hospital, Nungesser managed to shoot down forty-five German aircraft so that he ranked directly below René Fonck and George Guynemer on the French ace list. He was a determined fellow and during a convalescent leave for wounds received while with a bombing squadron, he flew and perfected his skill in fighter aircraft with the *Lafayette Escadrille.* On another occasion he refused the honorable discharge offered him because of his wounds and continued to fly. On the ground, however, he hobbled about with two canes and on some occasions had to be carried to his machine.

"The Leader of the Storks" by Henry Farré

USAF Art Collection

The Leader of the Storks

COMMANDANT BROCARD must have been a very impressive man. Captain René Fonck, the leading Allied fighter pilot, described in his book, *Ace of Aces*, his first meeting with Brocard on being assigned to the Storks:

> It is impossible to speak of the Storks without immediately invoking the glorious face of its illustrious chief. I felt like a little boy in presenting myself at the door of his barracks. He came toward me with hand outstretched.
>
> He was a robust fellow, with broad shoulders, massive and well-built, a Frenchman such as the old soil produced when nature truly succeeded in its work. One experiences the feeling of having before him a man and a powerful force at the same time. When he circulated among us, comrade and buddy, the most whimsical, the most reckless and the most independent feel, in spite of themselves, an impression of deep respect. Such is the way Major Brocard appeared to me from the first.
>
> He had four squadrons under his command; he was justly proud of them. They were the most magnificent in France. They always made the enemy withdraw before their onslaught. In skirmishes and combat they were first-rate in every respect. They were glorious at the very instant of combat.
>
> At the twilight of the Great War, they whirled above the fields of carnage until the end, with eyes red as fire, completely at ease during the attack. Major Brocard's Storks had 1,000 Boches to their credit.

"Escadrille Lafayette" Attacking a German Patrol Over the Champagne Sector

By the end of 1916 the French *escadrilles de chasse* began to trade in their Nieuport 17's for the sturdier Spad VII's. The *Escadrille Lafayette*, or N. 124, being an integral part of the French *Aviation Militaire* also received their Spad VII's. Mid-summer 1917 saw the Lafayette completely equipped with Spads resulting in their being redesignated SPA. 124. On February 18, 1918, the American 103rd Aero Squadron was organized from former members of the Lafayette Flying Corps who had accepted commissions as officers in the U.S. Air Service. They became the first American squadron to see action, but continued to fly on the French front and under French tactical control. They were also equipped with some of the 189 Spad VII's purchased by the United States the preceding December.

Vimnèra's painting shows the 103rd, which was still known as the "Lafayette Escadrille," in action against a German patrol of Albatroses over the Champagne front.

The Spads in the illustration still bear the French red, white, and blue cockade instead of the American red, blue, and white (see p. 78).

Single Combat Over Rheims

Lt. Charles Nungesser went in for macabre insignia on his aircraft. His Nieuport 24 bis bore, on both sides of the fuselage, a large black heart containing a white skull and crossbones, a coffin, and two candles (see p. 79). He used the same insignia on his Hanriot HD 1 during the war and on a "barnstorming" tour of the United States following the armistice.

Jokingly he would say that it was his own cracked skull and broken legs depicted in the insignia. Its design can be clearly seen in the watercolor on the side of his Nieuport 24 bis.

This practice of Nungesser's was unusual, in that most Allied aircraft wore distinctive squadron insignia and reserved their individuality for color and pattern designs. It is reminiscent, however, of the distinctive individual insignia on U.S. aircraft of World War II.

Even during his bomber days he had simple black skull and crossbones painted on the nose of his Voisin.

See page 34

"The Morane-Saulnier N" by Jack Leynnwood

See page 34

"Kazakov Scores for Russia" by B. Knight

See page 35

"The Eagle of Lille" by Gene Thomas

See page 35

"The Fokker Scourge" by B. Knight

See page 38

"The Eastern Central Power" by Jack Leynnwood

See page 45

"First Double for France" by Joseph A. Phelan

from Heroes and Aeroplanes of the Great War 1914–1918 *pub. by Grosset & Dunlap,* © *1966*

See page 38

"England's Answer to the Fokker Scourge" by B. Knight

See page 59

"A Double Victory for Guynemer" by A. Vimnèra

" 'Escadrille Lafayette' Attacking a German Patrol" by A. Vimnèra *See page 72*

See page 72

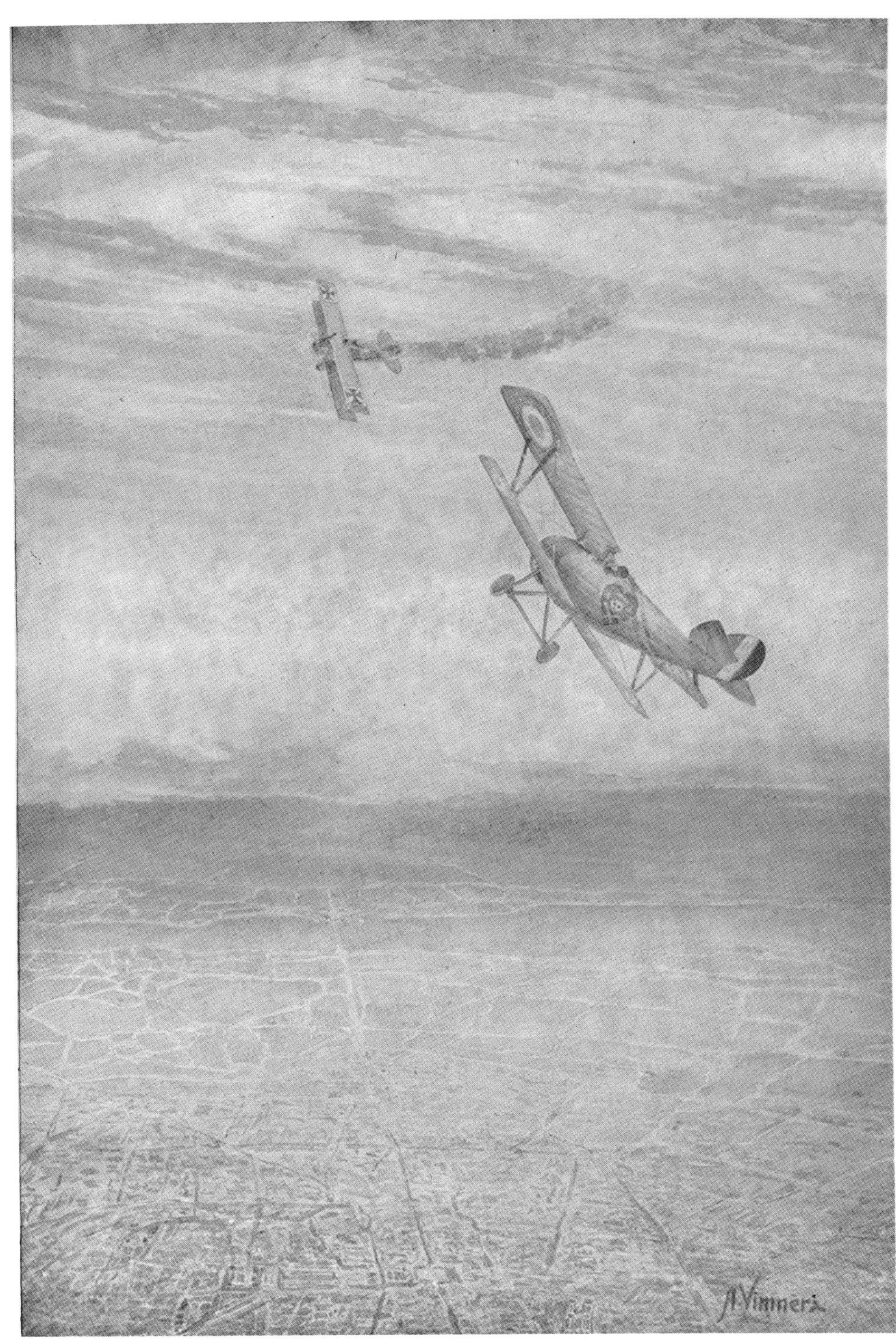

"Single Combat Over Rheims" by A. Vimnèra

See page 89

"Maneuvering for the Attack" by A. Vimnèra

See page 104

"Flight Companion of the Albatros"
by Gene Thomas

See page 101

"A Victory for 'Black Maria'" by Gene Thomas

"Pride of the Fatherland" by Joseph A. Phelan

from Heroes and Aeroplanes of the Great War 1914–1918 *pub. by Grosset & Dunlap, © 1966*

See page 104

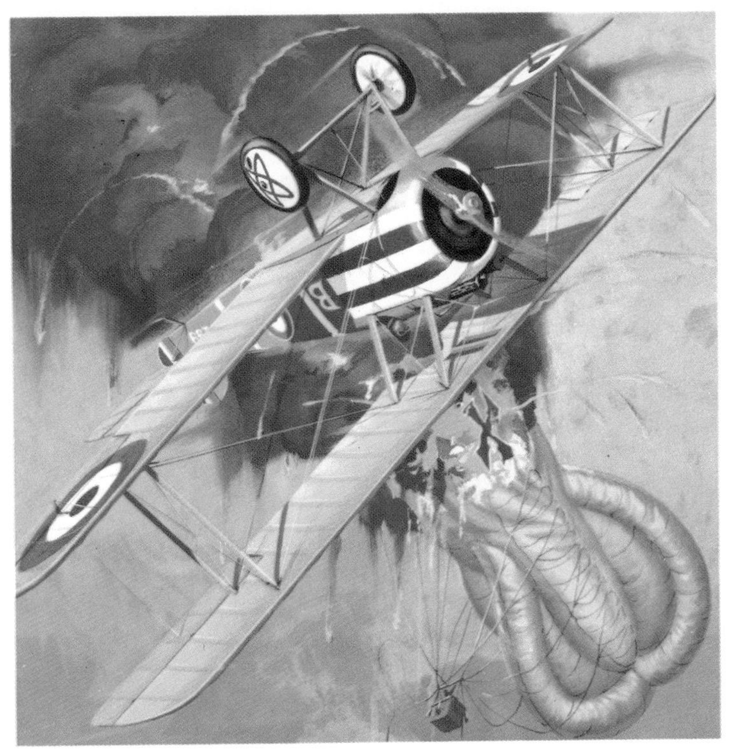

See page 108

"The 'Camel'" by Jack Leynnwood

See page 116

"The Best From Farnborough" by Jack Leynnwood

See page 117

"Americans With the Royal Flying Corps"
by Mort Künstler

See page 126

"An Alumnus of the 'Lafayette'" by Gene Thomas

See page 121

"The Wing-Stripper" by Gene Thomas

See page 127

See page 141

"Best Fighter of the War"
by Gene Thomas

"McKeever and the 'Brisfit' "
by Mort Künstler

See page 157

"Night Fighters Against the Giants" by Joseph A. Phelan

from Heroes and Aeroplanes of the Great War 1914–1918 *pub. by Grosset & Dunlap, © 1966*

See page 161

"A Seaplane Sinks the First Submarine" by Joseph A. Phelan

from Heroes and Aeroplanes of the Great War 1914–1918 *pub. by Grosset & Dunlap, © 1966*

"Captain René Fonck"
by Clyde A. Risley

Allied Ace-of-Aces

CAPTAIN RENÉ FONCK, who amassed a total of seventy-five confirmed victories (120 by his own count), was the Allied ace-of-aces of the First World War and, in fact, the leading surviving ace of both sides.

He was a remarkable flier and a skilled marksman. Fonck used very few bullets to bring down an enemy machine and, in contrast to Nungesser, was himself never touched by a German shot.

Major Charles J. Biddle, an American ace of that war and a former member of the *Escadrille Lafayette* and Spad 73 of the Storks, said that "when it came to shooting, Fonck was in a class to himself." In the Foreword to Fonck's autobiographical book, *Ace of Aces*, Biddle claimed that René Fonck was "easily the finest fighter pilot produced by the aviation service of any nation in World War I. His courage, flying ability, and especially his shooting, were simply superb."

THE SPAD VII, which he flew, was more than a match for the early Fokker bi-planes, which followed the *Eindekkers,* and for the Albatros D III, which had returned air superiority to the Germans.

Vimnèra's watercolor shows a Spad VII, with the advantage of height, about to pounce upon one of the Albatros D III's below it. The Spad VII in Farré's painting has just put the torch to a Fokker D IV (see p. 80).

"Spad 3 of *Les Cigognes*—Capt. Alfred Auger" by Henry Farré

USAF Art Collection

Spad 3 of Les Cigognes

LES CIGOGNES, or the "Storks," consisted of four fighter squadrons—the finest in the French *Armée de l'Air*. These were Spad No.'s 3, 26, 73, and 103. First of these was *Escadrille Spad 3* which included on its roster some of France's top aces. Among them were the legendary Georges Guynemer, *Père* Dorme, Mathieu de la Tour, Albert Deullin, Alfred Auger and Alfred Heurtaux. The latter two served successively as commanders of the squadrons. The two preceding aces, de la Tour and Deullin, went on to the command of other *Escadrilles* in the Group-Spad No.'s 26 and 73.

Captain Alfred Auger succeeded Commandant Brocard to the command of Spad No. 3, then designated *Escadrille N.3** because they flew Nieuport scouts, when Brocard was promoted to head the Storks.

* French squadrons were identified by the type of aircraft they flew. An *Escadrille* 38 flying Morane-Saulniers would be designed M.S. 38.

"Captain Alfred Heurtaux" by Henry Farré

USAF Art Collection

Captain Alfred Heurtaux

When Captain Auger died, Captain Alfred Heurtaux assumed command of Spad 3. He had joined the *Escadrille* when they were flying Nieuports and therefore bore the designation N.3, or Nieuport No. 3.

Heurtaux began his flying career as an observer. He had the misfortune of having a pilot who was accident prone and cracked up one plane after another. Heurtaux decided that if he was going to die in a crash he would rather do it himself and therefore requested pilot training. He learned to fly on the Bleriot X1, received his brevet on May 29, 1915, and was posted on M.S.38.

He so distinguished himself during the Battle of Verdun that he was assigned to the Storks–*Escadrille N.3.*

Under his command, and following re-equipment with the Spad VII, *Escadrille SPA.3* established a record unequaled during the war –200 enemy aircraft shot down in a period of six months.

"Captain Mathieu de la Tour of the Storks" by Henry Farré

USAF Art Collection

"Combat in a Circle at 6,500 Meters Altitude" by Henry Farré

USAF Art Collection

Captain Mathieu de La Tour of the Storks

SPAD NO. 26 was one of the four elite fighter squadrons that made up *Groupe de Combat No. 12,* better known as the Storks. Roland Garros, the first to shoot down an enemy aircraft by firing a machine gun through the propeller arc, had been a member of the squadron before he was forced down behind enemy lines and captured.

Captain Mathieu de la Tour, described by René Fonck as "the bravest of the brave," commanded Spad No. 26. Earlier he had been a member of the Stork squadron Spad No. 3. He was officially credited with nine confirmed victories.

THE TRICK in single-seater aerial combat was, and still is today, to get on to the tail of your adversary, stick to him like glue, and keep peppering him with a stream of machine gun fire aiming for the vital parts—motor, cockpit, gas tank or controls.

This tactic was effective against single-seater fighters. Two-seaters, however, were birds of a different feather. Most carried a sting in the rear, in the form of a flexible machine gun that could be handled by the observer in tractor-driven aircraft (as compared to the pusher type).

In this particular action, de la Tour did battle with an Albatros two-seater. It was armed with a flexible Parabellum machine gun in the rear.

The battle was fought at an altitude of 6,500 meters, approximately 7,040 yards or four miles.

"One Against Sixty" by Archibald Barnes

RCAF Collection

One Against Sixty

Major William Barker was a Canadian like his friend and post-war partner, Billy Bishop. His most remarkable exploit was a battle against sixty enemy aircraft, reminiscent of Werner Voss's fight against McCudden and his flight. The difference was that Barker fought against a greater number of the enemy—and he lived to tell the tale.

Barker, who had previously flown the Sopwith Camel in Italy against the Austrians, was flying a more advanced model called the Sopwith Snipe. He had been ordered back from Italy to England, but had wangled a few weeks tour of duty in France at the front. That duty was now completed and he was about to make the journey across the Channel to England. So reluctant was he to leave the action that he took a detour in the opposite direction, over the lines. Spotting an enemy two-seater he immediately attacked. But since it was expected that he was flying directly to England and would not engage in combat his telescopic sights had been removed. Barker was forced to close with the enemy and use the ordinary peep sight. This brought him into range of the rear observer who peppered him judiciously. Squinting through the peep sight Barker squeezed off a few well-placed bursts, blasting his adversary out of the sky.

While he had been focusing his attention on the two-seater, a Fokker fighter had fastened himself to Barker's tail and had smashed his right thigh with an explosive bullet. Although in extreme pain he outmaneuvered the Fokker and sent him spinning down in flames. Unconscious from loss of blood Barker, too, went down out of control. By some stroke of good fortune he revived, only to find himself in the midst of a flock of German aircraft that infantrymen and other eyewitnesses on the ground estimated to be more than sixty. They came at him from every angle and Barker banked, dived, twisted and turned, and every time a black cross came into sight he squeezed off a burst. He fought like a demon and struggled to keep conscious. Despite his efforts he lapsed into unconsciousness several more times, only to regain consciousness scant feet before he'd have crashed to his death.

"Someone up there must have liked him" because Billy Barker survived that epic one-sided battle to bring his Sopwith Snipe to a crash landing just inside the British lines. His aircraft was completely shot up and he took another explosive bullet in his elbow, but he had shot down five enemy planes.

Barker's tenacity, bravery, and skill in that fracas won him the Victoria Cross.

"The Sopwith Triplane" by Jo Kotula

The Sopwith Triplane

ONE OF THE most interesting machines to leave the prolific, creative aircraft "stable" of T.O.M. Sopwith was the Triplane. It was a change of pace in a great line of biplane fighting machines, including the Sopwith Pup, 1½ Strutter, Camel, Dolphin, and Snipe.

The Sopwith Triplane was the first successful three-tiered airplane and it served as the impetus, if not the model, for the Fokker DR 1 Triplane, which became famous as the mount of the great German Aces, Manfred *Freiherr* von Richthofen, Werner Voss, and Ernest Udet.

An interesting sidelight is the fact that the Sopwith Triplane served almost exclusively with squadrons of the RNAS, which got them by default. The RNAS had SPAD VII's on order but the RFC needed them badly. A plan was worked out where the SPAD's were diverted to the RFC and the RNAS got the "Tripes."

The RNAS did a magnificient job with the Sopwith Triplanes, and some of its officers, led by the intrepid Ray Collishaw, truly distinguished themselves.

" 'Black Flight' Leader" by Archibald Barnes

RCAF Collection

"Black Flight" Leader

Another member of that gallant contingent from Canada was Ray Collishaw who, like his countryman Billy Bishop, went on to distinguish himself in World War II as an Air Vice Marshal.

When the First World War broke out, Collishaw was serving as an officer in the Canadian merchant marine. He sailed for England and volunteered for duty in the Royal Naval Air Service. He got his wings in January 1916, was assigned to fly coastal patrols, and was an artillery spotter for coastal guns.

By early 1917, he had become a flight commander in No. 10 Naval Squadron, after having scored a number of victories. Equipped with the new Sopwith Triplane, Collishaw and his flight of Canadians (Flight Sub-Lieutenants Ellis Reid, Melville Alexander, Gerald Nash, and J. E. Sharman) became practically invincible even against von Richthofen's "Circus."

Each member of the flight gave his aircraft a name starting with "Black." They were "Black Sheep," "Black Prince," "Black Rodger," "Black Death," and Collishaw's "Black Maria" (see p. 81).

"The 'V-Strutter' " by John Steel

"The Albatros D V" by Mort Künstler

The "V-Strutter"

IF AN AWARD had been made to the most beautiful aircraft of the war it probably would have been given to the Albatros D III. Trim, neat, and beautifully streamlined, the D III was in a class by itself. Together with its predecessors, D I and D II, it had wrested control of the air from the Allies that had eventually been lost to the *Eindekker.*

The Albatros D III was the first of its line to have "V" struts which were said to have been copied from the Nieuport. It rapidly became the prime fighter in the Richthofen *Jagdgeschwader* and the other *Jastas.*

ENGLAND AND France did not sit idly by and leave the mastery of the skies over the Western Front to the Albatros D III. In short order they were turning out Sopwith Pups, SE 5a's and Spads. The German's in turn produced the Albatros D V and D Va as successors to the D III.

These later Albatros models, although more streamlined and with a fully rounded rudder, had a weakness in the wing structure and were a slight improvement, if at all, over the Albatros D III.

Flight Companion of the Albatros

ALTHOUGH ITS performance was not up to the standard of the Albatros fighters, the Pfalz D III was often grouped together with the Albatros in the German *Staffeln.*

The Pfalz D III resembled its Albatros mates very closely although differences could be readily noticed in its modified "V" strut—more rounded rudder, smaller more angular tail surface, and the lack of scalloping on the trailing edges of its wings (see p. 81).

Pride of the Fatherland

PERHAPS, HAD he lived, another great German ace might have rivaled von Richthofen for top honors. Lt. Werner Voss, son of a Jewish dyer from Krefeld, fought a most gallant and memorable battle, single-handedly in his silver blue Fokker triplane, against seven British S.E.5's flown by the cream of the Royal Flying Corps (RFC), including the great McCudden (see p. 82).

That "dog fight," shown in the painting to the right, was described in the recently republished book, *Flying Fury*, by Major James T. B. McCudden:

> We were just on the point of engaging six Albatros scouts away to our right, when we saw ahead of us, just above Poelcappelle, an S.E. half-spinning down, closely pursued by a silvery blue German triplane at very close range. The S.E. certainly looked very unhappy, so we changed our minds about attacking the six V-strutters, and went to the rescue of the unfortunate S.E.
>
> The Hun triplane was practically underneath our formation now, and so down we dived at a colossal speed. I went to the right, Rhys-Davids to the left, and we got behind the triplane together. The German pilot saw us and turned in a most disconcertingly quick manner, not a climbing nor Immelmann turn, but a sort of flat half-spin. By now the German triplane was in the middle of our formation, and its handling was wonderful to

behold. The pilot seemed to be firing at all of us simultaneously, and although I got behind him a second time, I could hardly stay there for a second. His movements were so quick and uncertain that none of us could hold him in sight at all for any decisive time.

I now got a good opportunity as he was coming towards me nose-on, and slightly underneath, and had apparently not seen me. I dropped my nose, got him well in my sight, and pressed both triggers. As soon as I fired, up came his nose at me, and I heard clack-clack-clack-clack, as his bullets passed close to me and through my wings. I distinctly noticed the red-yellow flashes from his parallel Spandau guns. As he flashed by me I caught a glimpse of a black head in the triplane with no hat at all.

By this time a red-nosed Albatros Scout had arrived, and was apparently doing its best to guard the triplane's tail, and it was well handled too. The formation of six Albatros scouts which we were going to attack at first stayed above us, and were prevented from diving on us by the arrival of a formation of Spads, whose leader apparently appreciated our position, and kept the six Albatroses otherwise engaged.

The triplane was still circling round in the midst of six S.E.'s who were all firing at it as opportunity offered, and at one time I noted the triplane in the apex of a cone of tracer bullets from at least five machine guns simultaneously, and each machine had two guns. By now the fighting was very low, and the red-nosed Albatros had gone down and out, but the triplane still remained. I had temporarily lost sight of the triplane whilst changing a drum of my Lewis gun, and when I next saw him he was very low, still being engaged by an S.E. marked 1, the pilot being Rhys-Davids. I noticed that the triplane's movements were very erratic, and then I saw him go into a fairly steep dive and so I continued to watch, and then saw the triplane hit the ground and disappear into a thousand fragments, for it seemed to me that it literally went to powder.

Strange to say, I was the only pilot who witnessed the triplane crash, for even Rhys-Davids, who finally shot it down, did not see its end.

It was now quite late, so we flew home to the aerodrome, and as long as I live I shall never forget my admiration for that German pilot, who single-handed fought seven of us for ten minutes, and also put some bullets through all of our machines. His flying was wonderful, his courage magnificent, and in my opinion he is the bravest German airman whom it has been my privilege to see fight."

"The Red Baron" by Clyde A. Risley

"The 'Tripehound' Scores" by Mort Künstler

The Red Baron

RITTMEISTER MANFRED Freiherr von Richthofen's name is probably known by more Americans today than it was during his heyday.

He came from a family of the lesser nobility and his title of Baron was bestowed upon him by his British adversaries rather than by his "Fatherland" or Kaiser. More correctly his title was *Freiherr*. His military rank *Rittmeister* was a Cavalry one and was the equivalent of Captain, or in the other German military services, *Hauptmann*.

Like Lt. Colonel Billy Bishop of the RAF, he had been a cavalryman, in a Uhlan regiment, earlier in the war, and transferred to the air service. Still like Bishop, his first air assignment was as an observer.

Finally von Richthofen was successful in his request for pilot training and graduated as a two-seater flier. He fought in the battle of Verdun in his lumbering two-seater and even succeeded in shooting down a Nieuport. Von Richthofen yearned for a single-seater and had a little opportunity to fly a *Fokker Eindekker* in between his observation and bombing flights at the Russian front.

A visit to the Baron's squadron by Oswald Boelcke got him a transfer to Boelcke's *Jagdstaffel*, or fighter squadron. Boelcke was the idol of the Fatherland and his squadron was the elite of the Imperial German Flying Service, only to be eclipsed later by von Richthofen's own *Jagdstaffel 11* and his group, *Jagdgeschwader 1*.

Boelcke became von Richthofen's mentor and under the tutelage of his master, the Baron, mounted in an Albatros D II, scored his first confirmed victory on September 17, 1916.

THE FOKKER Dr I Triplane, inspired by the British Sopwith Triplane, was designed by Fokker's chief aeronautical engineer, Reinhold Platz. Its wingspan was about three feet shorter than the English triplane and their fuselages were about the same length. The German machine had less horsepower, was slower, and its endurance was one hour and fifteen minutes less than its British counterpart. These deficiencies notwithstanding, the Fokker Triplane was a great fighter. Matched against the Sopwith Camel, which was a later model than the Sopwith Triplane, the Dr I used to advantage its great agility and its unusually rapid rate of climb.

Following the tradition established when Fokker presented his first models of the *Eindekker* to Boelcke and Immelmann, the first examples of the Fokker Triplane went to aces Werner Voss and Manfred von Richthofen. Tragically, both lost their lives in this machine.

The "Camel"

ALTHOUGH THE S.E. 5 was preferred by many of the British and American aces over the Sopwith Camel, the fact still stands that more enemy aircraft were destroyed by the Camel than by any other type of aircraft during World War I (see p. 83).

George A. Vaughn, Jr., the American ace who flew only British aircraft compared the two fighters:

> . . . the Camel had the reputation among some RAF personnel of being a "death trap"—sure to spin in from a right turn made too close to the ground. This of course was a pure myth, although the Camel was a rather tricky and very sensitive airplane to fly. To dispel the rumor, the British authorities arranged for an expert stunt pilot named Armstrong to tour the various training fields—putting his Camel through all kinds of acrobatic maneuvers just a few feet off the ground. I believe he was killed eventually—but not in a Camel.
>
> A little experience with the Camel and its delicate control responses proved it to be an exceptionally satisfactory craft in many respects. It was inherently unstable (rigged so tail-heavy that it would nose up and stall immediately if flown hands off) but it was highly maneuverable, climbed well at low and medium altitudes, and when properly handled was a most effective weapon in close in air combat at these altitudes. The S.E.5, somewhat less maneuverable, was a bit faster, a more stable gun platform, faster in the dive, and capable of higher altitudes. Some of our present-day pilots, accustomed to pressurized cockpits or oxygen to breathe, look somewhat askance when told that we occasionally used the S.E.5's up around 20,000 feet, with open cockpits and no oxygen.

Captain A. Roy Brown, a Canadian, was flying a Sopwith Camel in the engagement in which the Red Baron was shot down.

The Royal Navy's Camels

THE STANDARD Sopwith Camel F 1 was modified for naval service and was designated the 2F 1.

It had a smaller wingspan, designed to take up less space on an "aircraft carrier," and a detachable rear fuselage for the same purpose. The other principle difference was in the armament. The 2F 1 had a Lewis gun mounted on the upper wing and a single synchronizer Vickers forward of the cockpit to replace the twin Vickers of the standard F 1 model.

A Royal Naval Air Service Sopwith Camel 2F 1 is credited with shooting down the last Zeppelin in the First World War.

"The Royal Navy's Camel" by Clayton Knight
USAF Art Collection

“Death of the Baron” by Charles H. Hubbell

© 1947 Thompson Products, Inc.

Death of the Baron

On the morning of April 21, 1918, Captain A. Roy Brown was not feeling too well. His stomach, which had been bothering him for some time, had been acting up again. Despite his illness he took off in command of his flight of Sopwith Camels. Before departing he warned Lt. Wilfred R. May, a fellow Canadian who had not seen action yet, not to do anything rash.

Soon they spotted two Allied RE 8 two-seaters under attack by a flight of Fokker Triplanes. Brown immediately dived followed by his flight. Somehow in the dog fight that followed, Lt. May became separated from his buddies. Looking about Brown saw May being followed closely by an all-red triplane. He banked hard to the left to go to May's rescue.

Today, more than 50 years after the death of Manfred von Richthofen, not too much more light has been shed on the details of his demise. In fact the situation has probably become more confused.

Brown, who is officially credited with bringing down the Baron, did not claim that he had shot him down. Although he did not know the identity of the pilot, he had claimed victory over a red German machine at that time and place.

Various other claims have been made including that of an Australian machine gunner. This also could be a valid claim because all three aircraft, May's, von Richthofen's, and Brown's, came within 100 feet of the ground and the Allied infantrymen opened up with everything they had at the enemy triplane.

Despite all of the firing concentrated on the red plane only one bullet entered the Baron's body. That solitary shot killed him but who actually fired it is still unknown.

It is interesting to note that the Red Baron claimed no Americans among his eighty victims. However, the explanation is a reasonable one. He fought opposite the British and all his victories were scored against Englishmen or members of what was then the British Empire. Although some Americans flew with the RFC and its successor RAF, far more flew with the French before the U.S. entered the war. American-trained aero squadrons flew their first patrols and Lt. Doug Campbell shot down the first enemy aircraft by a U.S. trained aviator barely a week before the Baron fought his last battle and came down in his little red triplane on the Allied side of the line, dead at the stick.

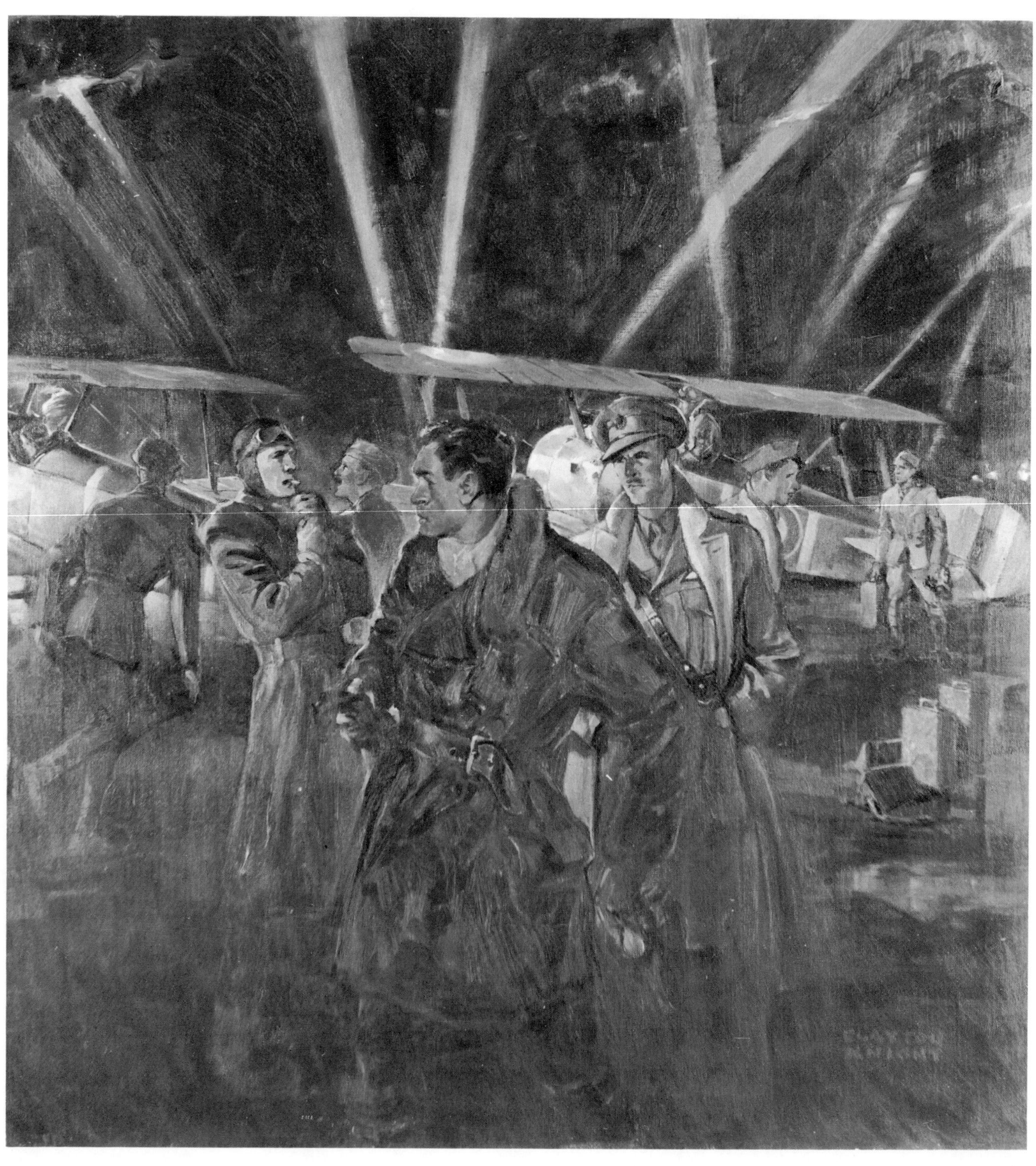

"The First Night Fighters" by Clayton Knight
USAF Art Collection

The First Night Fighters

ARTIST CLAYTON Knight's painting graphically depicts a night scene of the fighter aerodrome.

Although the night fighter Sopwith Camels were modified for their particular mission, the changes were not as drastic as those performed on the Royal Navy's model 2F 1's. The modifications on the night fighter Camels centered mainly around the armament.

Night fighter pilots were temporarily blinded by the flashes from their twin Vickers guns. Although it lasted only a few seconds, it was long enough for them to lose their quarry or to put them at a disadvantage; therefore twin Lewis guns mounted on the center section of the upper wing were substituted for the twin Vickers guns. In some cases the cockpit was moved back for greater ease in handling the guns and a faired headrest was provided.

Night fighter Camels, despite their modifications, still retained the F 1 designation.

"Dog Fight" by Clayton Knight

USAF Art Collection

Dog Fight

To most people the mention of aerial combat in World War I conjures up a vision of a dog fight—hundreds of airplanes of different types, and of different nationalities, milling about in the sky, each one striving to position himself on the tail of his adversary or on some other vulnerable spot. The vision, in full color, saw the multi-hued aircraft whirling around; red, white, and blue cockades chasing black crosses and vice versa.

The scene also included aircraft disintegrating in mid-air, others trailing smoke, and some going down in a burst of flame.

This was, in effect, what an aerial dog fight really was except that they did not occur that frequently, nor were the numbers of participating aircraft that great.

The Best From Farnborough

JUST OUTSIDE of London, at Farnborough, was the site of the Royal Aircraft Factory. Here government-employed aeronautical engineers and aircraft designers competed with private industry (Vickers, De Haviland, Bristol, Sopwith, and others) to satisfy the voracious appetites of the Royal Flying Corps, Royal Naval Air Service, and their successor the Royal Air Force, for more and better aircraft.

The Royal Aircraft Factory designed the B.E., F.E., R.E., and S.E. series. B.E. stood for "Blériot Experimental," F.E. for "Fighter Experimental," R.E. for "Reconnaissance Experimental," and S.E. for "Scouting Experimental."

By far the best product of the Royal Aircraft Factory was the fifth in the Scouting Experimental series, the famous S.E.5. Three of the top British aces—Bishop, Mannock, and McCudden scored most of their victories in this type aircraft (see p. 83).

American ace George A. Vaughn, Jr., who trained and fought with the RFC and RAF was rather apprehensive at being transferred from a squadron equipped with the S.E.5 to one that flew the Sopwith Camel, although it meant a promotion. In his Foreword to the new edition of Captain Duncan Grinnell-Milne's *Wind in the Wires,* Vaughn stated:

> After some two months with the 17th, I found I had become quite fond of the Camels, and had survived a number of pretty tough scraps in them, but given a free choice, I believe I still would have picked the S.E.5 as my all-round preference.

Americans with the Royal Flying Corps

When the call to arms rang out on the entrance of the United States into the First World War, fired by the feats of Fonck, McCudden, von Richthofen, and others, a number of young Americans rushed in to join the fledgling U.S. Army Signal Corps Air Service.

They were given some of their training in the United States and were then sent overseas, presumably to Italy, for further training. Aboard ship they were taught Italian by a peppery little ex-Congressman from New York—Captain Fiorello H. LaGuardia.

Although La Guardia and some other officers went on to Italy, a group of some 200 cadets remained in England. Among them were Elliott White Springs, George A. Vaughn, Jr., and others of that Princeton University contingent of twenty-five that learned to fly and soloed on Curtiss "Jennies" even before their enlistment.

The part played by Springs and a number of his buddies is dramatically told in the book, *War Birds.* They flew British aircraft—S.E.5's and Sopwith Camels—in Royal Flying Corps squadrons. Springs and his gang flew with Billy Bishop in No. 85 Squadron, RFC. Later, Springs was named Commanding Officer of the U.S. 148th Aero Squadron which was equipped with the British Camel and which operated under RAF Command. Near the close of the war the 148th was assigned to the U.S. Fourth Pursuit Group under the command of Major Charles J. Biddle.

Springs became America's fifth ranking ace with twelve confirmed victories. The painting depicts his victory over a Fokker D VII in an S.E.5a (see p. 84).

"Vaughn Bursts a Balloon" by Charles H. Hubbell

Vaughn Bursts a Balloon

Brooklyn-born Lt. George A. Vaughn, Jr., a member of the Princeton group that trained with the British, was assigned to No. 84 Squadron RAF about the same time that Springs joined Billy Bishop's No. 85 Squadron. He flew the S.E.5a, scoring six victories in it. Among these was the destruction of the German balloon illustrated here.

The citation for the British Distinguished Flying Cross described the action:

> For conspicuous bravery in attacking enemy aircraft. On August 25th, 1918, while on offensive patrol, he attacked an enemy kite balloon near Hem. Closing to within point blank range he fired upon it so that it burst into flames and was destroyed. Shortly afterward, observing an enemy two-seater over Maricourt he attacked it, shooting it down from a height of 500 feet so that it completely crashed.

Four days after flaming the balloon, Vaughn was transferred to the U.S. 17th Aero Squadron, which also fought on the British front and was under English operational control. Here Vaughn flew Sopwith Camels and added seven more victories to his score, for a total of thirteen.

In his Foreword to Captain Duncan Grinnell-Milne's *Wind in the Wires*, Vaughn pays tribute to Americans who flew with the RAF:

> The relatively small War Birds group probably saw at least as much combat service as any other World War I pilots who wore the American uniforms, yet they never flew a U.S.-built aircraft over the lines, or flew over an American army on the ground. I am sure they felt "the bond" even more keenly than the British.

There were also a number of other Americans who flew and fought in British squadrons but who never wore the American uniform because they did not enlist in or transfer to the U.S. Air Service, preferring to remain with the RAF.

Nineteen of these unsung heroes racked up rather impressive scores that would have put them at the top of the U.S. list of fighter aces. Instead, their names appear only on the British list.

Among them are Captain W. C. Lambert with 22 confirmed victories; Flight Sub-Lieutenant John J. Malone, 20; Captain F. L. Hale, 18; Captain A. T. Iaccaci, 18; Captain W. Gillette, 16; Lt. C. T. Warman, 15; Captain F. L. Libby, 14; Lt. P. T. Iaccaci, 11; and Lt. L. L. Richardson, 10.

"First For the Yanks" by Charles H. Hubbell

First for the Yanks

ALTHOUGH AMERICANS had enrolled as much as two years earlier in the ranks of the *Lafayette Escadrille* and the Royal Flying Corps (RFC), it was not until March 19, 1918,that American-trained pilots flew and fought in U.S. squadrons under American command with their own red, blue, and white national cockade.

Major Raoul Lufbery, highest scoring American in the *Lafayette* and newly commissioned in the U.S. Air Service, led the first patrol of the 94th "Hat-in-the-Ring" Squadron but they did not engage the enemy. On April 14, 1918,he took neophyte aviators Lts. Eddie Rickenbacker and Reed Chambers over the lines but that flight too was uneventful. That same day Lts. Alan Winslow and Doug Campbell remained at the field on standby alert. They took off in their Nieuport 28's on being notified that two enemy aircraft were in the vicinity, and met them over the 94th's field. Winslow, who had also flown with the *Lafayette Escadrille*, dispatched his adversary at once. He was followed immediately by Campbell who brought down his opponent to become the first American-trained pilot to score a victory against the enemy.

The Wing-Stripper

THE NIEUPORT 28 was a direct descendant of the excellent French-designed and French-built Nieuports 11 and 17. It was, however, the first non-"Vee strutter" in the line.

It was the first fighter aircraft furnished to most of the newly formed American squadrons on the French and American fronts. It was also the aircraft in which the 94th "Hat-in-the-Ring" squadron flew its first patrols and gained its first victories. Lt. Douglas Campbell, in a Nieuport 28, became the first American-trained pilot to down an enemy machine, and Eddie Rickenbacker scored his first "wins" in it.

The Nieuport 28, however, had the unfortunate tendency of stripping the fabric from its wings in a dive. For this reason it was replaced in the AEF squadrons by the stronger Spad XIII.

Lt. Jimmy Meissner, Brooklyn-born like George Vaughn, found himself in this unfortunate position, with the fabric torn from his wings, on two occasions and barely escaped with his life. Eddie Rickenbacker saved Meissner's hide on the second one, and bagged two Albatroses in the attempt (see p. 85).

" 'Rick' Nails a 'Drachen' " by Mort Künstler

"The American Ace-of-Aces" by Howard Chandler Christy

The American Ace-of-Aces

Captain Edward V. Rickenbacker gained the title of American ace-of-aces in the short span of six months, from April 29 to October 30, 1918. More remarkable, however, is the fact that his twenty-six victories were actually amassed during a period of only two-and-a-half months—from April 29 to May 30, and from September 14 to October 30. The balance of the time he spent in the hospital recuperating from a serious mastoid operation.

He also had the honor of commanding America's leading and most colorful fighting unit—the 94th Aero Squadron, better known as the "Hat-in-the-Ring" Squadron because of the colorful insignia painted on the sides of its aircraft.

The French-built Spad XIII captured the imagination of the American public during the First World War. This popularity was not without justification, however, since the Spad was widely celebrated in fact as well as fiction. And following the unhappy Nieuport 28, with which they were first equipped, it became the principal fighter aircraft flown by the American pursuit squadrons.

It was a colorful plane and the favorite of the leading American aces. Eddie Rickenbacker, Frank Luke, Doug Campbell, and Reed Chambers, among others, flew it in combat and with great success. Together with the Sopwith Camels, S.E.5's and Fokker D VII's, they constituted the finest aircraft to emerge from World War I.

There were dissenting votes, however. Major Charles J. Biddle, a veteran of the Storks, the *Lafayette Escadrille*, and wartime commander of the U.S. Fourth Pursuit Group, tells in the latest edition of his book, *Fighting Airman—The Way of the Eagle,* of his preference for the earlier model Spad VII.

The painting shows "Captain Eddie" pulling away from his eleventh victory at Sivry-sur-Meuse, on September 28, 1918. In all, Rickenbacker destroyed four balloons—two in the air and two on the ground.

"A Double for Rickenbacker" by Charles H. Hubbell

A Double for Rickenbacker

REPEATING A feat he had already performed twice before and would do again three more times, Captain Edward V. Rickenbacker on October 3, 1918, shot down two German two-seaters on the same patrol.

He brought down a Rumpler at 16:40 * and twenty-seven minutes later engaged in the action depicted here, bringing down the enemy LVG C V for his fifteenth victory.

"Rick's" other doubles took place on September 25, October 2, October 10, October 27, and October 30, 1918. In the action fought on October 10th, he shot down two Fokkers practically simultaneously and twenty days later he destroyed a balloon and a Fokker within five minutes.

* 4:40 P.M. on the military 24-hour clock.

An Alumnus of the "Lafayette"

LT. DAVID E. Putnam, a direct lineal descendant of Revolutionary War General Israel Putnam, left Harvard in his sophomore year to sail for France and enlist in the French *Service de l'Aviation.*

He had completed his flight training and was at the front assigned to *Escadrille SPA 94* before the United States entered the war. Although he never flew with the *Lafayette Escadrille* he was considered part of the Lafayette Flying Corps, as were all Americans who fought in French squadrons. Putnam also served with SPA. 156 (when they flew Nieuports, and then the Morane-Saulnier Parasol), and with SPA. 38.

On June 8, 1918, he was commissioned a First Lieutenant in the U.S. Air Service and shortly thereafter was given command of the American 139th Aero Squadron.

The painting shows Putnam in his Spad XIII replete with the U.S. red, blue, and white cockades and the Greek God Mercury insignia of the 139th Aero Squadron, bearing down on the tail of a Fokker D VII (see p. 84).

Before his untimely death on September 13, 1918, in a battle against eight Fokkers, Putnam was officially credited with downing twelve enemy aircraft although he claimed more. He had been awarded the U.S. Distinguished Service Cross, the French *Légion d' Honneur, Medaille Militaire,* and *Croix de Guerre.*

"Best Fighter of the War"

ALTHOUGH THE Fokker D VIII was the last in the line of fighters manufactured by the Dutch aeronautical engineer, Anthony Fokker, and gave promise of being a great scrapper, it appeared in action only in the last few days of the war. Its predecessor, the Fokker D VII, left no doubt, however, about its ability as a combat aircraft (see p. 86).

This angular fighter with the narrow "N" struts recaptured the prestige and awe of the earlier Fokker *Eindekkers*, despite the fact that the Fokker Triplane also had an excellent reputation. Baron von Richthofen was shot down the very month (April 1918) that the Fokker D VII began to be supplied to his *Jagdgeschwader* 1. As was the practice in the Imperial German Air Service, the first to receive the new aircraft were the top aces in the elite *Jastas*. Within five months, forty-eight fighter squadrons had been equipped with more than 800 D VII's.

A backhanded compliment was paid to the Fokker D VII by the Allies who mentioned it specifically in the Armistice.

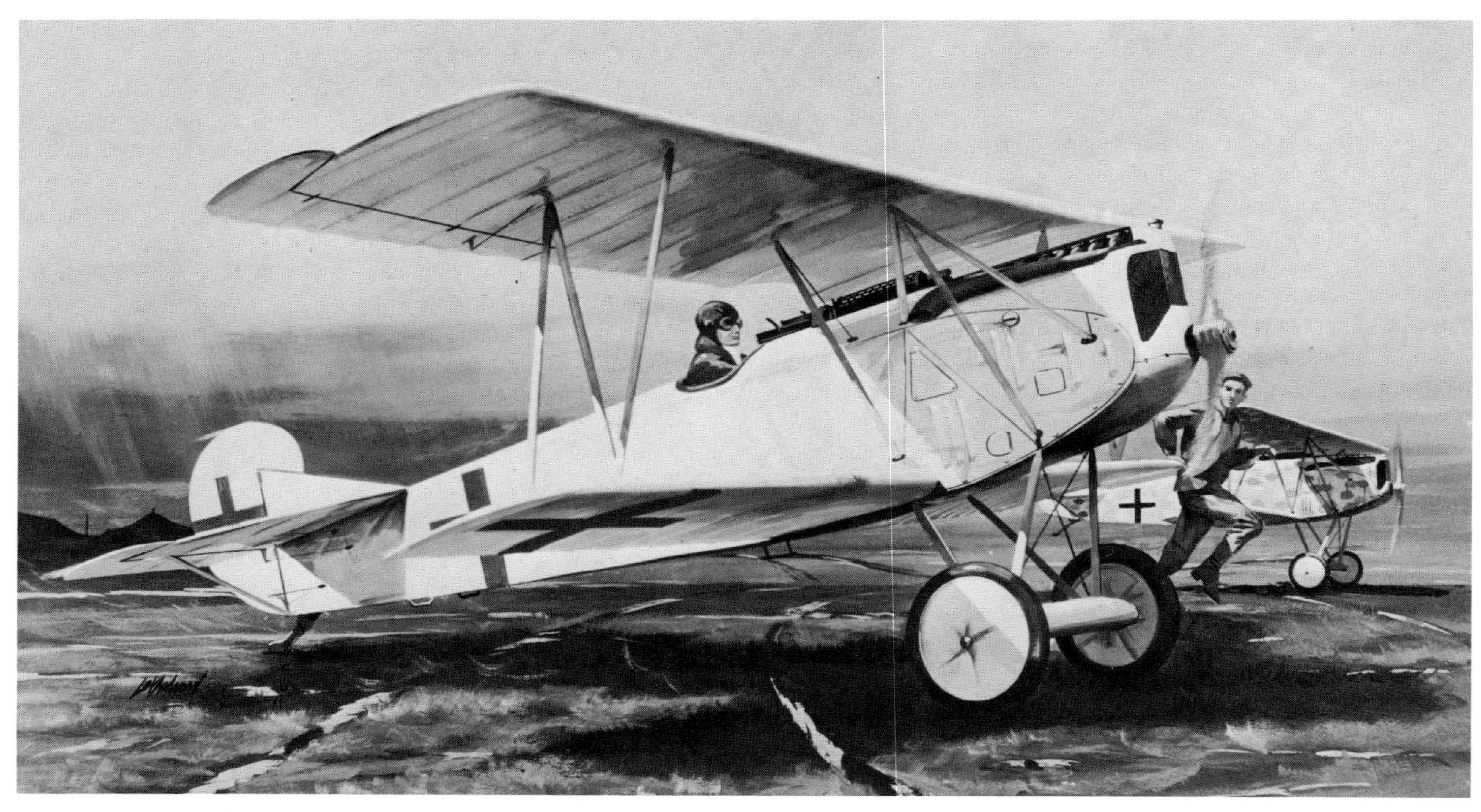

"Black Knave in a White Fokker" by Jack Leynnwood
© 1944 Revell, Inc.

Black Knave in a White Fokker

GROUP CAPTAIN Johnny Johnson, top RAF and Allied ace of the Second World War, classed the Red Baron as the best of World War I. He ranked him over René Fonck, the leading Allied ace of the First War who had seventy-five confirmed victories and was a superb marksman who always returned from a fight completely unscathed. Other runners-up were the top British aces, "Mick" Mannock, Billy Bishop, and Jim McCudden.

But Group Captain Johnson not only took flying and fighting ability into account when he made his choice, but also he considered leadership. The Red Baron was an outstanding leader. His "Flying Circus" was a most efficient fighting force, although colorful. He trained and created other aces, and in his all-red scout he led first his own squadron—*Jasta* 11, and then the elite "Richthofen Group" of squadrons—*Jagdgeschwader* 1.

Proof of his leadership ability may be found in the fact that on his death, command of J.G.1 (*Jagdgeschwader* 1) fell to Hermann Goering, of later Nazi infamy. Once again "Fat Hermann" proved to be a loser! Under his leadership the once powerful "Richthofen Group" was so cut up and mauled in combat that it had to be withdrawn from the front.

It is interesting to note that Goering was credited with twenty-two official victories, less than half of the forty-eight earned by Werner Voss, who had a Jewish heritage. And Goering only had three more than *Leutnant* Wilhelm Frankel, another Jewish ace whose record he and Hitler tried unsuccessfully to destroy when he became head of the Nazi *Luftwaffe.* (It did not look good to have a Jewish hero.) All three; Frankel, Voss, and Goering won their country's highest award for valor, the *Pour le Mérite*—sometimes called the "Blue Max."

Goering's all-white Fokker D VII is shown in the painting.

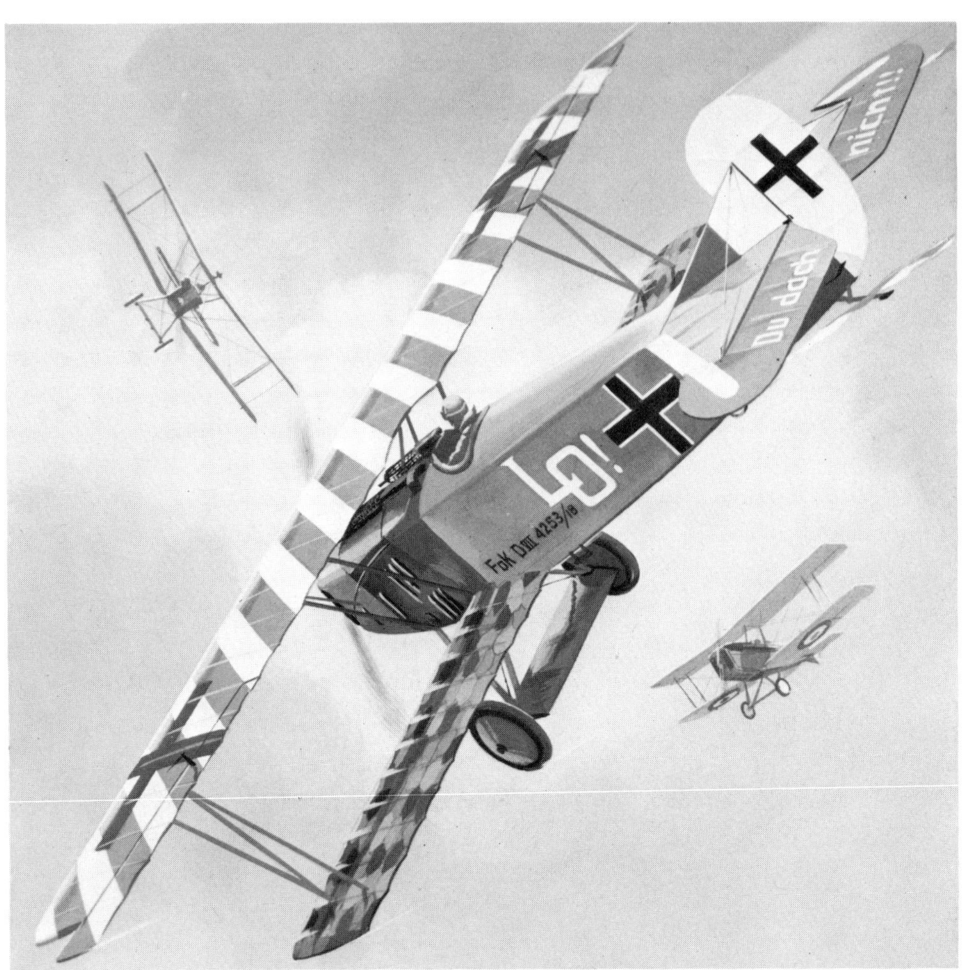

"Du Doch Nicht!!" by Jack Leynnwood

"Ace of the Iron Cross" by Roger Ulanoff

Ace of the Iron Cross

OBERLEUTNANT* ERNST Udet was the leading surviving ace of the Imperial German Air Service and his sixty-two victories placed him second only to Manfred von Richthofen (see p. 107).

Udet, who began the war as a motorcyclist, transferred to the air service and became a pilot. He flew as an enlisted man because the Germans, like the French and English, did not necessarily give commissions to their pilots. (The United States, on the other hand, awarded officer's commissions to all of its pilots. Most of the Americans who flew with the Lafayette Flying Corps held the French ranks of Sergeant or Corporal but received commissioned ranks in the U.S. Air Service.)

Later on, Udet received his commission and by the end of the war commanded a fighter squadron in the Red Baron's *Jagdgeschwader* 1. He was a stunt pilot in the 1920's and '30's, and a General in the *Luftwaffe* during World War II. He did not get along with Hermann Goering, his former fellow fighter pilot of 1914-18 who had become the Nazi Chief of the *Luftwaffe*. Udet was made a scapegoat and was forced to commit suicide.

His Fokker D VII had diagonal red and white stripes on the top wing, his girl friend "Lo's" name on the side of the fuselage, and the tail bore the taunting inscription "*Du doch nicht*!!!—"Certainly not you!!!"

* First Lieutenant.

"Too Late!" by Jo Kotula

Too Late!

THE HIGH-WINGED monoplane Fokker D VIII was the last of that great fighter family produced by the "Flying Dutchman," Anthony Fokker in the First World War. It arrived on the Western Front less than one month before the close of the war and gave promise of rivaling its bi-plane predecessor, the Fokker D VII, as the greatest fighter aircraft of the First World War. It was more maneuverable than the D VII but less so than the Fokker Triplane.

In a dog-fight just five days prior to the Armistice, Baron von Richthofen's old *staffel*, flying Fokker D VIII's, shot down three Spads, the last Allied aircraft to be destroyed in the Great War.

In reverting to the single wing design and the rotary engine, Fokker had gone full circle, harking back to his *Eindekker* series introduced in 1915. At that time Allied aircraft were no match for the "Fokker Scourge" and their synchronized Spandau machines guns, until the introduction of the French Nieuport 11 *Bébé* and the British pusher-type D. H. 2.

"Voisin" by Henry Farré

USAF Art Collection

"Aeroplanes Being Guarded by Sentry" by Henry Farré

USAF Art Collection

BOMBER AND RECONNAISSANCE AIRCRAFT

(Multiple Engine and/or Crew)

Voisin Airplane

At the start of the war Voisin models 1 and 2, also known as Type L, went into action as artillery observation aircraft in four French *escadrilles.* Within a few months they were converted to daylight bombers. Although these pusher aircraft were rather weak-looking, they were actually well constructed and sturdy for their time. While most aircraft of the period were constructed of wood, they had steel airframes.

The Voisin 3, or Type LA, was also known as the Voisin *Canon* because of the Hotchkiss gun mounted in the forward cockpit for the observer.

The war was barely two months old when a Voisin LA scored the first victory for France. More than 1,000 of this model were built, serving with the British, Russian, Belgian, and Italian air services as well as with the French. A later model 3, which had the engine raised for greater thrust, was designated LA.S and when a more powerful engine was added it became known as the Type 5 LA.S.

While the Voisin LA.S had been initially employed on daylight missions, it became a night bomber in September of 1915. It was used in this capacity practically until the end of the war. One of the missions recorded on canvas by Farré was the bombing of Sablons at Metz.

The "Voisin Peugeot," or model LA.P (type 8), was a later edition which entered service toward the end of 1916. It was powered by a stronger 220-hp Peugeot engine and was easily distinguished by its twin streamlined fuel tanks slung under the top wing. Although 1,123 of them were built not too many saw service.

"Return of the Body of Capt. Féquant" by Henry Farré
USAF Art Collection

"Salute to the Hero" by Henry Farré
USAF Art Collection

Return of the Body of Captain Féquant

THE TWO paintings by Farré show, in sequence, a Voisin LA.S in flight with the body of the observer, Captain Féquant, slumped over the cockpit, and the sad scene at the aerodrome after landing.

Captain Féquant had been killed in an aerial engagement with a German aircraft, and the pilot brought him home. Captain Féquant's brother was one of those present when the Voisin landed. Farré was also a witness to this event and was so touched by it that he was compelled to paint it.

"Harry Tate"

"The 'Brisfit' " by Clayton Knight
USAF Art Collection

"Harry Tate"

THE RE 8, or "Harry Tate" as it was affectionately called by those who flew it, was a product of the British Royal Aircraft Factory at Farnborough. Although it was designed at Farnborough, seven British manufacturers produced close to 4,100 duplicates of the RE 8. Numerically it was the most popular British two-seater on the western Front.

The Harry Tate was replaced by the superior Bristol Fighter. It had served long beyond its normal tour of duty and became a victim of the more advanced enemy fighters. Despite this fact, quite a few were still in service at the end of the war.

The "Brisfit"

THE BRISTOL Fighter was an "odd ball." It broke the tradition that all fighter planes had to be single-seaters. The tradition, however, was not one of long standing. Aerial warfare was not even three years old when the Bristol Fighter first appeared on the scene, in early 1917.

But the "Brisfit" was not an instant success. In fact, on April 5, 1917, they were so badly mauled in combat against the Red Baron and some of his wingmates that only two of a flight of six returned. The fault lay in tactics and not in the aircraft. Pilots had been flying the Bristol Fighter like a conventional two-seater, relying on the observer and his Lewis gun in the rear when they got into a scrap. When it was flown like a single-seater scout, with the pilot using his fixed synchronized Vickers it became a formidable weapon—a fighter with an extra sting in the tail.

"Chalk Up Another for the Bristol Fighter" by Charles H. Hubbell

McKeever and the "Brisfit"

CAPTAIN ANDREW E. McKeever, another Canadian, was probably the best known of the Bristol Fighter pilots, if not of all two-seater pilots. Most of his thirty victories were gained in the redoubtable two-seater which he flew like a single-seater. This did not deny his observer, Lt. L. F. Powell, his crack at the enemy since he too became an ace in his own right, one of the few non-pilots to make it. Together they were an invincible team.

McKeever was first assigned to the Brisfit when he was posted to No. 11 Squadron RFC in May 1917. He took to it "like a duck takes to water." As an infantryman, before transferring to the Royal Flying Corps he had gained a reputation as an expert marksman. He carried over this skill to his handling of the single synchronized Vickers machine gun mounted in front of his cockpit.

Neither single-seaters nor two-seaters proved a match for McKeever. Mort Künstler's painting shows McKeever in his Bristol Fighter bringing down what appears to be an Albatros single-seater, and Charles Hubbell's rendition depicts his destruction of a German two-seater DFW C V (see p. 86).

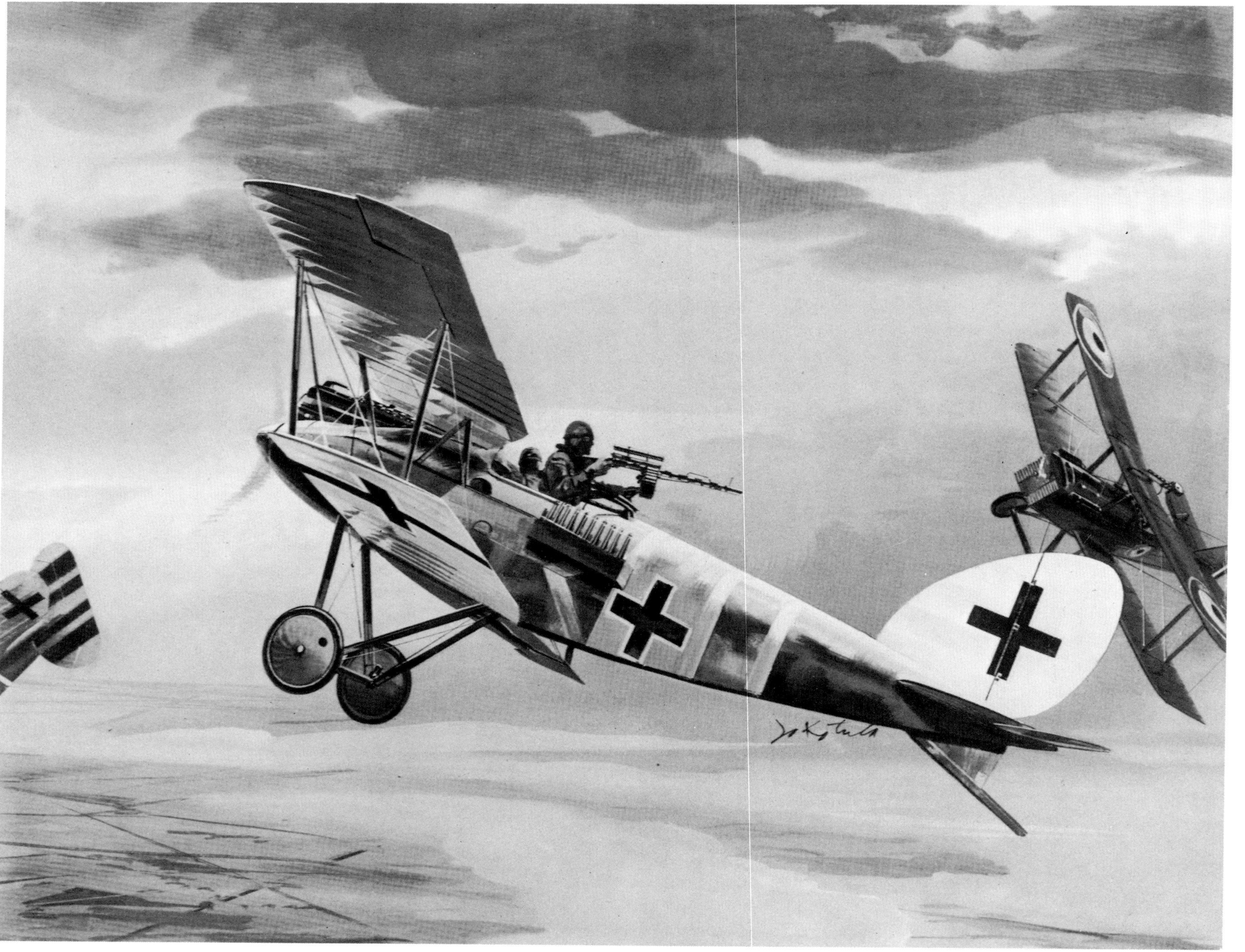

"The Germans Had a Two-Seater Fighter Too" by Jo Kotula

The Germans Had a Two-Seater Fighter Too

LIKE THE Bristol Fighter, the Halberstadt CL II two-seater was built like a fighter. It was the first of the German C-class, heavy armed two-seaters designed for greater maneuverability, and hence lighter. (The "L" in its designation stood for *leicht,* the German word for "light.")

The CL II was a powerful, versatile aircraft often used in trench strafing or harassing the enemy infantry.

The painting shows the Halberstadt CL II tangling with a British SE 5.

"The Albatros Two-Seater" by Jo Kotula

The Albatros Two-Seater

THE ALBATROS factory, famous for its single-seat fighters, produced two-seaters for the Imperial German Air Service even before it manufactured the smaller scouts. In fact, Manfred von Richthofen, Ernst Udet, Hermann Goering, and others who were to become leading fighter aces flew Albatros two-seaters before they were transferred to fighters.

First of the Albatros two-seaters were the B I and B II, both of which were pre-war machines. Typical of the time, neither of these aircraft were armed. When the German High Command created the C-class of armed two-seaters, the *Albatros Werke G.m.b.H.* produced the Albatros C I, which was, in effect, "a souped up" B II with a flexible Parabellum machine gun in the rear. The improved model C III, pictured here, later carried a fixed Spandau in the front for the pilot, in addition to the observer's weapon.

"Jenny" by Gene Thomas

"Jenny"

NICKNAMED "JENNY" because of the "JN" combination in its designation, the Curtiss JN became well known as a trainer. There were several variants of this aircraft but the JN 4 model was probably the most popular model, and close to 6,500 were built.

The Jenny was the aircraft on which most of the American-trained pilots "cut their teeth," and it was also used by the RFC and RNAS.

The Curtiss JN4 also had a career in post-war days as a "barnstormer." The wildly decorated Jenny, illustrated by Gene Thomas, was one of those barnstormers.

"Air Battle Over the Shell Holes" by Clayton Knight

USAF Art Collection

"Under Attack" by Charles H. Hubbell

Air Battle Over the Shell Holes

ONLY FOUR American airmen earned our nation's highest decoration for valor during the First World War. Medals of Honor were bestowed on Lt. Frank Luke, Jr., the Arizona "Balloon Buster"; Capt. Eddie Rickenbacker; and Lts. Harold E. Goettler and Erwin R. Bleckley. Rickenbacker was the only one who lived to receive his award.

While Luke and Rickenbacker were fighter pilots and flew Spad XIII's, Goettler and Bleckley, pilot and observer, made up the crew of a two-seater D.H.4. Their Medals of Honor were given for the risks they took repeatedly flying at tree-top level to locate and drop much needed food and medical supplies to the beleagured "Lost Battalion," a mission in which both lost their lives.

The plane they flew, the De Havilland 4, was known as "The Flaming Coffin," and although of British design it was American-built. It was in fact the only American-built aircraft to see action. At the time of the armistice there were 196 American-constructed D.H. 4's at the front.

Many thought that the D.H. 4 was a mighty poor choice for the United States and that the French Salmson was a much superior aircraft. In reference to this situation, General Billy Mitchell stated: "Instead of the fine and suitable French airplanes specified, they had adopted the British De Havilland."

Hubbell's fine illustration shows a formation of American D.H. 4's defending themselves against a trap set by a gaggle of Fokker D VII's, and Clayton Knight's shows a couple of Fokker Triplanes on the tail of a D.H. 4.

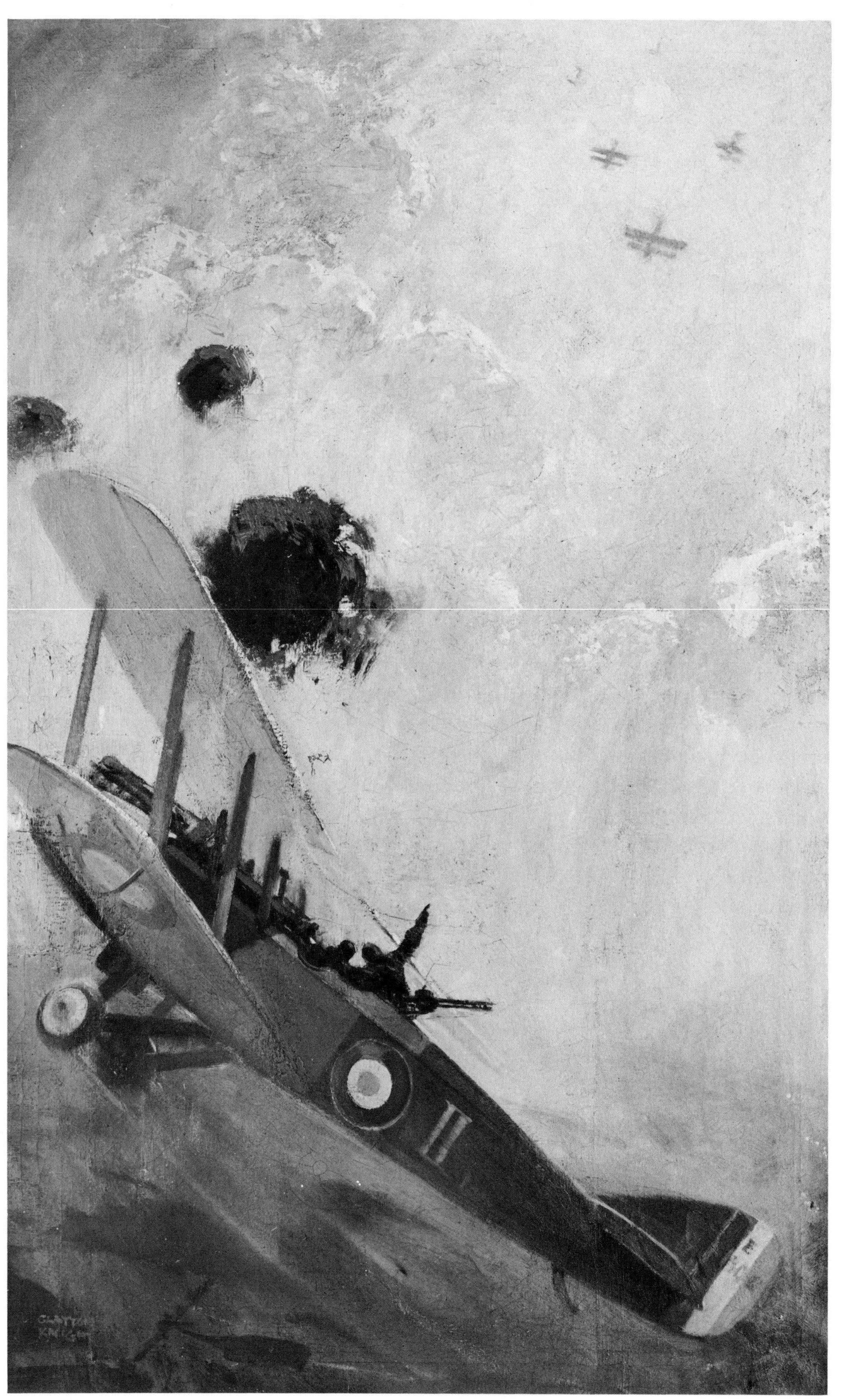

"Out of the Sun" by Clayton Knight

USAF Art Collection

Out of the Sun

EARLY IN the war, fighter pilots learned the trick of having the sun behind them while waiting for their prey. As anyone knows, you cannot look into the sun without being blinded, if only temporarily. A skilled fighter pilot could pounce upon an unsuspecting foe by diving on him from out of the sun.

Clayton Knight's painting shows a British DH 9 about to be attacked by a gaggle of Fokker D VII's. The observer, tapping the pilot on the shoulder, is pointing to them swooping down out of the sun.

"A French Bomber" by Jo Kotula

© Aurora Plastics Corp.

A French Bomber

One of the better two-seater French aircraft developed during the war was the Breguet 14. It was produced in two models, the 14A2 and the 14B2. The former was a reconnaissance aircraft and the latter a bomber.

The United States purchased 290 of them, and 43 were in service at the Front with AEF squadrons at the time of the Armistice.

"An English Bomber" by Jo Kotula

An English Bomber

The De Havilland 10, a twin-engine day-bomber, never saw action in World War I since only a small number of them were delivered to the Royal Air Force shortly before the cessation of hostilities. It was the largest aircraft designed by Geoffrey de Havilland and produced by Airco (Aircraft Manufacturing Co.), as well as the last Airco machine to see service in the 1914-18 War.

Following the war, they flew the mail from England to the British Army of Occupation in Germany, and served in India on the Northwest Frontier.

"Wir Fahren Gegen Engeland" by Jo Kotula

"Wir Fahren Gegen Engeland"

Best known of the German World War I bombers was the Gotha. It was manufactured by a company which had been in the wagon business—the *Gothaer Wagonfabrik A.G.* It produced its first G-class (*Grossflugzeug*, or large airplane) early in 1915. This was the Gotha G I.

First of the "English Raiders" were the Gotha G IV's which made their first attack on "perfidious Albion" in May 1917. The raids were made in daylight for a period of four months after which they continued their missions at night. At that time the improved G V model began to replace it. The Gotha G V continued its nocturnal raids on England in May 1918, a year after the attacks had begun.

Night Fighters Against the Giants

Greatest of the German bombers were the R-class (*Riesenflugzeug*, or giant airplanes). These were built and/or designed by Siemens-Schuckert and *Zeppelin Werke Staaken.* The latter, an offshoot of the Gotha Company, was under the direction of Count Zeppelin, the same one who had designed and built the giant dirigibles that had also played a part in the bombing of England.

These R-planes were truly the giants of their day with wingspans ranging to 140 feet. (For purposes of comparison, the World War II Flying Fortress only had a wingspan of 104 feet.) They were powered by up to six engines driving combinations of tractor and pusher propellers, and carried a crew of seven. Five machine gun positions were well placed to cover all angles of the mammoth aircraft.

Joe Phelan dramatically and colorfully illustrated two Staaken R XVI's under attack by night fighters. The event illustrated here took place on August 10, 1918. The Staaken in the foreground, number R 43, was the only R-plane brought down by fighter action (see p. 87).

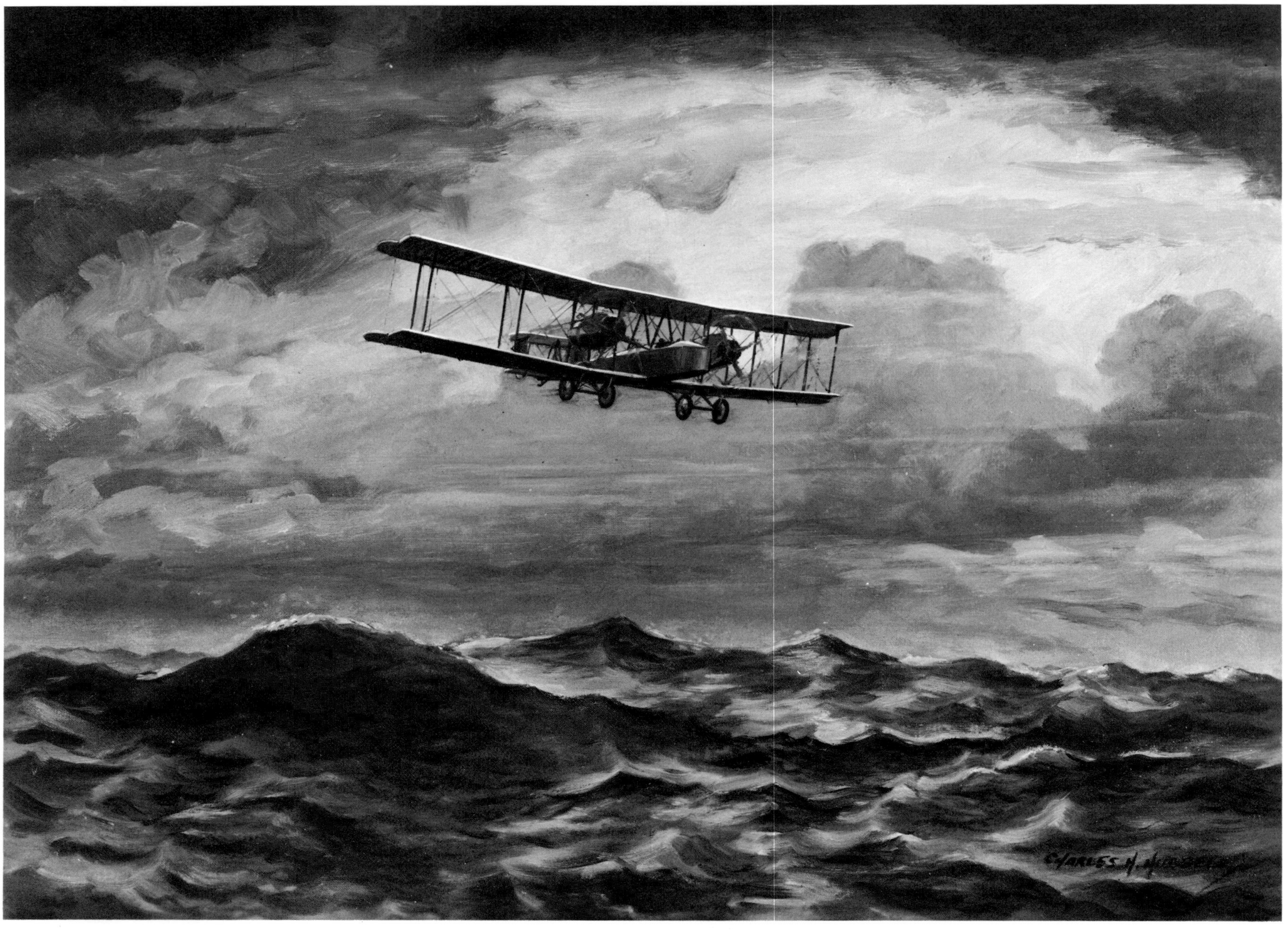

"A War Veteran Makes the First Non-Stop Transatlantic Flight" by Charles H. Hubbell

A War Veteran Makes the First Non-Stop Transatlantic Flight

DESIGNED PRIMARILY to bomb Berlin from bases in France, the Vickers Vimy, like the De Havilland 10, arrived on the scene too late to see action. Like the DH 10, however, the twin-engine bomber distinguished itself in a civilian capacity following the war.

On June 14-15, 1919, Captain John Alcock, of Manchester, England, and Lt. Arthur W. Brown, born of American parents in Glasgow, Scotland, made the first non-stop transatlantic crossing to win the $50,000 London *Daily Mail* prize. They successfully flew the 1,936 mile span of ocean between St. Johns, Newfoundland, and Clifden in Northern Ireland. Although unhurt, they landed nose-down in a bog which had looked like a meadow from the air.

During November and December of that same year two Australian brothers, Captain Ross Smith and Lt. Keith Smith flew more than 11,000 miles from Australia to England, also in a modified Vickers Vimy.

"Seaplane Under Attack" by Henry Farré
USAF Art Collection

"Rescue at Sea" by Henry Farré
USAF Art Collection

FLYING BOATS AND FLOATPLANES

Seaplanes Under Attack and Rescue at Sea

The Franco British Aviation Company (FBA) built the FBA Type H flying boats shown in these three paintings by Farré. The Type H was preceded by the FBA Lévêque, named after its designer, which was produced in 1913. This model served with the Danish and Austrian Naval Air Services but not with the French until the outbreak of the war. An improved model, Type B, appeared in 1915, followed by the Type C the next year, which in turn led to the Type H.

FBA flying boats served with the British RNAS, the Russians, the French; the Italians alone built close to 1,000 of the FBA Type H.

A Seaplane Sinks the First Submarine

The French *Aviation Militaire* had its *Bébé* in the Nieuport 11 and the British Royal Naval Air Service had its Sopwith Baby Floatplane (see p. 88). This little seaplane was a direct descendant of the modified Sopwith Tabloid, rigged with twin-floats, that had won the Schneider Cup at the air races held in Monaco during April 1914, a scant few months before the start of hostilities.

The Sopwith Baby, together with the French FBA Type H Flying Boat and other amphibian aircraft, did a magnificent job in seeking out enemy submarines.

Flying patrols over seemingly endless stretches of water seeking out enemy submarines and searching for mines must have been a boring task indeed. Lt. David S. Ingalls, an American Naval Aviator, had been assigned to the Allied naval base at the port of Dunkirk in France as a member of a naval coastal patrol squadron. Bored with the routine, he wangled permission to fly Sopwith Camels, during his off-duty hours, with the nearby No. 213 Squadron RAF. He flew missions for three months before he scored his first victory, and then within a few weeks he shot down four more enemy aircraft to become America's only naval ace of World War I.

"Short Type 184 Floatplane" by Joseph A. Phelan

Short Type 184 Floatplane

The Short Type 184 Floatplane was designed specifically for the job of carrying and launching a torpedo from the air. It was the first such aircraft and true to its mission. On August 12, 1915, it sank a Turkish merchant vessel to become the first airplane to destroy a ship from the air by means of a torpedo.

Like most naval flying machines, the Short 184 had folding wings and was designed to serve aboard seaplane carriers. It was, in a manner of speaking, a direct lineal ancestor of the Fairey "Swordfish" which did such a magnificent job as a torpedo aircraft in the Second World War.

Being naval aircraft, the Sopwith Baby, Short Type 184 Floatplanes, and the FBA Type H Flying Boat performed missions in support of their sea-going mates. It was perfectly natural to assign such aircraft the bombing of an enemy-held port, the destruction of its harbor facilities and harassment of shipping, and the sinking of ships to bottle up the harbor.

British Royal Naval Sopwith Baby's and Short 184's attacked the Belgian port of Ostend in 1916, and French FBA Type H Flying Boats struck at the Mole and Zeebruge in the same manner.

BIOGRAPHICAL SKETCHES OF THE ARTISTS

Archibald Barnes

(Page 100)

A CANADIAN artist, Archibald Barnes, did the portraits of two of Canada's top First World War aces, Lt. Colonel William Barker and Air Vice Marshal Raymond Collishaw. Little more, however, is known about Barnes.

Howard Chandler Christy

(Page 122)

BORN IN 1873, Howard Chandler Christy became one of America's most noted illustrators. He is best known for his "Christy Girl" magazine illustrations and posters. Christy also painted portraits and is represented in this volume by his heroic painting of Captain Eddie Rickenbacker. He died in 1952.

Henry Farré

(Pages 26, 42, 44, 50, 52, 54, 60, 62, 68, 70, 90, 92, 94, 120, 134, 136, 160)

WHEN WAR broke out in August of 1914, Henry Farré was many miles away in Argentina. He immediately sailed for France aboard the French liner *Lutetia*, which was shadowed across the Atlantic by the German warship *Cape Trafalgar.*

On arrival in France, Farré attempted to get into active service but was told to wait until his class was called up. Finally he prevailed and was assigned the dual duty of serving as an orderly to an officer friend and as an artist-painter. His duty was "to paint certain phases of action so as to immortalize on canvas true pictures of fighting in the field," for the French Army Museum. Since the officer whom he was serving as orderly was a pilot in a bomber squadron, Farré became one of the first combat artists to cover aviation activities. He was later commissioned an officer.

From covering bombing missions, Farré went on to a Naval squadron, and then painted scenes at aviation schools and of fighter aviation (including the *Lafayette Escadrille*). He also painted portraits of the leading aces.

Farré actually flew with the French 1st Bombardment Squadron and with the naval aviators, and was present at the raid on Zeebrugge. During one flight his plane was attacked by a German Rumpler but Lt. Navarre came to the rescue, in his bright red Nieuport *Bébé,* and downed the enemy.

This collection of Farré paintings of aviation in the First World War was donated to the U.S. Air Force by Laurence Rockefeller.

Charles H. Hubbell

(Pages 20, 22, 24, 28, 30, 32, 36, 46, 58, 66, 110, 118, 124, 140, 148, 158)

A RESIDENT of Cleveland, Charles H. Hubbell is a noted aviation artist, historian, and writer. He is probably best known for his colorful historical aviation paintings that have illustrated the calendars of TRW, Inc. (Thompson-Ramo-Woolridge, formerly the Thompson Aviation Co.) each month since January 1941. Some of these excellent paintings are presented in this book.

Hubbell has a studio at the Western Reserve Historical Society in Cleveland.

Brian Knight

(Pages 73, 75, 77)

BRIAN KNIGHT is an English artist who did some of the box cover art for Revell plastic model airplane kits that were manufactured in Great Britain. Some of these are illustrated here.

He was born in 1926 at Reading, in the county of Berkshire. He is married and lives in the "New Forest" of Hampshire.

Knight was educated at Wilson Senior School and later at Reading University, where he studied with Marcus Adams. He also attended evening classes in Technical Drawing after leaving school.

He was a member of the design staff at Miles Aircraft Ltd., at Woodley Aerodrome, Berkshire, during the last World War.

Later he created the Illustration Section at the Atomic Energy Research Authority, Harwell, Berkshire, where he met his wife, who also was employed by the Authority in the drawing office.

Knight spent two years as a Studio Manager for a big London art studio, and has been a free-lance artist for the past ten years. One of his clients is Revell (Great Britain) Ltd.

Clayton Knight

(Pages 109, 112, 114, 138, 148, 150)

A PART OF World War I aviation history himself, Clayton Knight sailed for Europe together with Elliot White Springs, Larry Calahan, and the rest of that group of "aviation cadets" immortalized in the book *War Birds.* En route they were under the command of Captain Fiorello H. LaGuardia who taught them Italian on board the ship as they were being sent to Italy for flight training. However, the orders were changed and most of the group remained in England and trained with the RAF. While Springs and Calahan were assigned to fighters, Knight flew two-seaters.

During the Second World War, before the U.S. entered the conflict, Knight served as chairman of a committee that actively recruited young Americans as aviation cadets for the RAF and training in Canada.

He did the drawings for *War Birds.* He wrote and illustrated the book *Lifeline in the Sky,* as well as a number of other books which he wrote together with his wife. The illustrations used in this volume are part of the USAF Art Collection and are used with the permission of the Air Force.

Morton Künstler

(Pages 84, 86, 102, 106, 122)

After graduating from Pratt Institute in 1950, Mort Künstler began his career as a free-lance illustrator. He has done more than 1,500 illustrations for advertising, books, and magazines, including *Boy's Life, Saturday Evening Post, National Geographic, Sports Afield* and *Outdoor Life*. He has also done box cover art for Renwal, a manufacturer of model airplane kits. Some of his Renwal illustrations are in this book. His work is realistic in style and the subject matter is generally adventure or historical.

Künstler was sent by the Society of Illustrators to Puerto Rico to do paintings of Ramey Air Force Base which are now in the permanent collection of the Air Force museum. He has been awarded two citations of merit from the Society of Illustrators and has held a one-man show at the Society gallery.

During his stay in Mexico, from 1961 to 1963, he did portraits and many paintings of Mexican life. Künstler lives on Long Island in Oyster Bay Cove, N.Y., with his wife and three children.

Jack Leynnwood

(Pages 56, 73, 75, 83, 128, 130)

Born in Los Angeles, California, Jack Leynnwood studied at the Art Center School. During World War II he served as a fighter pilot with the U.S. Army Air Force and flew P-40 *Warhawks* and P-38 *Lightnings*. He began his art career doing posters while in the Air Corps. Currently he is a free-lance illustrator in Playa Del Rey where he concentrates on illustrations and painting for industrial concerns, advertising agencies and national magazines. Leynnwood also does specialized-packaging illustrations for Revell, Inc., a number of which are featured in this volume. He has participated in the U.S. Air Force Historical Art Program and a number of his paintings are on exhibit in Washington, D.C., and at the Air Force Academy in Colorado Springs. He has exhibited at the Art Directors' Club and Society of Illustrators in Los Angeles.

Joseph A. Phelan

(Pages 64, 66, 76, 82, 87, 88, 162)

Phelan is author of the book *Heroes and Aeroplanes*, published by Grosset & Dunlap. In addition to writing the text, he did the illustrations and designed the book.

He also designed and painted the aircraft illustrations for the dust jackets of the new editions of *Ace of Aces* by René Fonck, *Winged Warfare* by Billy Bishop, *Fighting Airman—The Way of the Eagle* by Charles Biddle, *Flying Fury* by James McCudden, *Wind in the Wires* by Grinnell-Milne, *The Red Baron* by Von Richthofen, *Knight of the Iron Cross* by Ernst Udet, and others of the "Air Combat Classics" series.

His interest in the aero-history of the Great War began when he sketched air duels in his elementary school notebooks. His interest heightened while he served in the Pacific Theatre during World War II as a U.S. Navy illustrator, and led him to become a member of that dedicated group of World War I enthusiasts, the Cross and Cockade Society.

A graduate of Cooper Union Art School, Phelan was the art director for a New York City advertising agency. Recently he went into business for himself as a free-lance artist. He is married, has a son and two daughters, and lives in Hartsdale, New York.

Clyde A. Risley

(Pages 51, 89, 106)

CLYDE A. RISLEY became interested in model soldiers for their artistic expression some twenty years ago, when his art training from the High School of Music and Art and Pratt Institute of New York led him to become interested in military uniforms and creating miniature figures. A veteran of the Army Air Force in World War II, Risley returned to civilian life and into the advertising field, where he was an art director before joining William Imrie to form Imrie/Risley Miniatures. His work as a military artist has been seen by collectors for many years through the Society of Illustrators, and in his contributions to "Military Uniforms in America," a series of colored plates published by the Company of Military Historians, which recently honored him by selecting him a Fellow of the Company. His free time is devoted to the collection of eighteenth-century weapons and accouterments, as well as uniform research. He drew six pen-and-ink portraits of the aces exclusively for this volume.

Eugene G. Thomas

(Pages 40, 74, 81, 84, 85, 86, 146)

GENE THOMAS was born and grew up in the Bronx, N.Y. All through his childhood he was preoccupied with airplanes and spent his spare time building and flying models.

After two years in the Air Force, he studied illustration and then began his free-lance career. Gradually his interest turned from model planes to the real thing and not only did he learn to fly, but he also acquired and is rebuilding a 1930 Alexander Eaglerock biplane.

During this time, his art and research assignments have included aircraft paintings and photographs for *Flying* and *Air Progress* magazines, Renwal and Sterling models, as well as industrial illustrations for many well-known corporations.

At present Mr. Thomas and his wife operate their own art studio in Huntington, N.Y., and he is also an instructor at the School of Visual Arts. He is an active member of the Antique Airplane Association and the Aviation/Space Writers Association.

Roger Ulanoff

(Page 130)

BORN ON Long Island, this creative young man has been able to pack a great deal of excitement and adventure into his short 21 years. His experience has ranged from seaman in the U.S. Merchant Marine on the North European run to advertising-agency television-commercial production.

As an artist, his college professors speak of him as a young man with a great deal of promise. He won first prize in a graphics art contest and he is represented in this volume by a woodcut of Ernst Udet, *Ace of the Iron Cross.*

Presently he is turning his artistic talents to film and TV production, his field of specialization, at Temple University.

A. Vimnèra

(Pages 77, 78, 79, 80)

Four watercolors depicting, in action, the *Lafayette Escadrille*; the French ace, Charles Nungesser; Georges Guynemer scoring a double victory; and a Spad maneuvering for an attack against a flight of German Albatroses were painted by Vimnèra for the two-volume set of *The Lafayette Flying Corps*. These books were written and edited by Charles Nordhoff and James Norman Hall (former members of the "Lafayette," later commissioned as flying officers in the neophyte U.S. Air Service), who are best known for the book *Mutiny on the Bounty*. *The Lafayette Flying Corps* was originally published in 1920,and for years has been an extremely rare and costly collectors' item. In 1964,Cornell Jaray of Kennikat Press in Port Washington, N.Y., republished an extremely limited edition,using the original plates.

BIBLIOGRAPHY

Biddle, Charles J., *Fighting Airman-The Way of the Eagle,* Doubleday & Co., 1968

Bishop, William A., *Winged Warfare,* Doubleday & Co., 1967

Bowers, Peter M., *Forgotten Fighters and Experimental Aircraft of the U.S. Army: 1918–1941,* Arco Publishing Co., 1971

————, *Forgotten Fighters and Experimental Aircraft of the U.S. Navy: 1918–1941,* Arco Publishing Co., 1971

Coppens, Willy, *Flying in Flanders,* Ace Books, 1971

Farré, Henry., *Skyfighters of France,* Houghton Mifflin, 1918

Fonck, René, *Ace of Aces,* Doubleday & Co., 1967

Grinnell-Milne, Duncan, *Wind in the Wires,* Doubleday & Co., 1968

Groh, Richard, *Fifty Famous Fighter Aircraft,* Arco Publishing Co., 1968

Hall and Nordhoff, *The Lafayette Flying Corps,* Kennikat Press, 1964

Harleyford Publications (published in the U.S. by Aero Publishers):

Air Aces of the 1914–1918 War, 1959.

Aircraft of the 1914–1918 War, 1954

Fighter Aircraft of the 1914–1918 War, 1960

Marine Aircraft of the 1914–1918 War, 1966

Reconnaissance and Bomber Aircraft of the 1914–1918 War, 1962

Hythe, Viscount, *Naval Annual 1913,* Arco Publishing Co., 1970

Jane, Fred T., Ed., *Jane's All the World's Aircraft, 1913,* Arco Publishing Co., 1969

————, *Jane's All the World's Aircraft, 1919,* Arco Publishing Co., 1969

McCudden, James T. B., *Flying Fury,* Doubleday & Co., 1968

Morgan, Len and R. P. Shannon, *The Planes the Aces Flew,* Arco Publishing Co., 1964

Munson, Kenneth, *Fighters 1914–19,* Macmillan, 1968

————, *Bombers 1914–19,* Macmillan, 1968

————, *Warplanes of Yesteryear,* Arco Publishing Co., 1966

Palmer, Henry R., Jr., *The Seaplanes,* Arco Publishing Co., 1965

Phelan, Joseph A., *Heroes and Aeroplanes of the Great War 1914–1918,* Grosset & Dunlap, 1966

Taylor, John W. R., *Pictorial History of the RAF, Volume I: 1918–1939,* Arco Publishing Co., 1969

Udet, Ernst, *Ace of the Iron Cross,* Doubleday & Co., 1970

Ulanoff, Stanley M., *Fighter Pilot,* Doubleday & Co., 1962

————, *Bombs Away,* Doubleday & Co., 1971

————, *Illustrated Guide to U.S. Missiles and Rockets,* Doubleday & Co. 1959, 1962

Von Richthofen, Manfred, *The Red Baron,* Doubleday & Co., 1969

Whitehouse, Arch, *Heroes of the Sunlit Sky,* Doubleday & Co., 1967